MUSIC

TECHNIQUES, STYLES, INSTRUMENTS, AND PRACTICE

EDITED BY
RUSSELL KUHTZ

Britannica®
Educational Publishing
IN ASSOCIATION WITH

ROSEN
EDUCATIONAL SERVICES

Published in 2017 by Britannica Educational Publishing (a trademark of Encyclopædia Britannica, Inc.) in association with The Rosen Publishing Group, Inc.
29 East 21st Street, New York, NY 10010

Distributed exclusively by Rosen Publishing.
To see additional Britannica Educational Publishing titles, go to rosenpublishing.com.

First Edition

Britannica Educational Publishing
J.E. Luebering: Executive Director, Core Editorial
Anthony L. Green: Editor, Compton's by Britannica

Rosen Publishing
Kathy Campbell: Senior Editor
Nelson Sá: Art Director
Michael Moy: Designer
Cindy Reiman: Photography Manager
Nicole Baker: Photo Researcher
Introduction and supplementary material by Daniel E. Harmon

Library of Congress Cataloging-in-Publication Data

Names: Kuhtz, Russell.
Title: Music : techniques, styles, instruments, and practice / edited by Russell Kuhtz.
Description: First edition. | New York : Britannica Educational Publishing : in association with The Rosen Publishing Group, [2017] | Series: Britannica's practical guide to the arts | Includes biblio-graphical references and index.
Identifiers: LCCN 2015046634 | ISBN 9781680483727 (library bound : alk. paper)
Subjects: LCSH: Music--History and criticism--Juvenile literature.
Classification: LCC ML3928 .K84 2016 | DDC 781--dc23
LC record available at http://lccn.loc.gov/2015046634

Manufactured in China

CHAPTER THREE

CHAPTER FOUR

CHAPTER FIVE

CHAPTER SIX

Throbbing music emanates through the brick walls of a concert hall. It is merely noise to the ears of uninterested passersby. To young enthusiasts inside, though, it is invigorating and provocative. The heavy metal band onstage blends electric guitar, bass guitar, drums, and electronic keyboards to produce a unique, driving sound with metallic precision. It is a tour de force of modern instrumentation, ramped up to eardrum-piercing decibels. Above it, a vocalist shrills dark lyrics—a morose message of romantic passion mingled with despair.

In another part of the city at the same moment, a very different sound is having a similarly sobering effect on its listeners. A symphony orchestra sets the audience on edge with the dramatic opening chords of Beethoven's *Symphony No. 5: dah-dah-dah-DAH. . . . dah-dah-dah-DAH. . . .* According to Beethoven's secretary, the composer's intention was to musically depict "fate knocking at the door." *Symphony No. 5,*

The Pioneer High School band performs at an awards ceremony in Ann Arbor, Michigan, in 2015. Researchers have found that music education can improve young people's learning in English and mathematics.

composed in a minor key and dubbed the "Symphony of Death," has been adapted by musicians in rock, disco, and other genres to create ominous moods. It has become well known around the globe since it first was performed two centuries ago.

Half a world away, people sing, clap, and dance to the rhythms of *djembe* and *konkoni* drums at a tribal ceremony in Zimbabwe. Here, the subject is not at all sinister. The drums are enlivening a wedding celebration.

In Japan, families and friends gather for their children's violin recital. The young musicians render increasingly complex compositions with seemingly effortless confidence. For the finale, they unite, smiling and swaying as they play a grand waltz. The performers are ages five and six. The professional quality of their presentation—execution, feeling, demeanor—is stunning.

A street musician in London is busking—performing on a sidewalk for donations. She has mastered the bouzouki, a modern, eight-string variation of an ancient Greek instrument. Her repertoire is diverse, ranging from wild East European gypsy dances to Scottish reels. She also sings. Citizens and tourists stop to listen and place handsome tips in her instrument case in appreciation.

The sounds produced in these performances are strikingly different. Still, they all share key features that are common to most forms of music.

1. They each represent music of a particular style and genre.
2. Each genre is performed on certain types of instruments. In these instances, instrumentation involves electric/metal, symphonic, wooden drums, bowed strings, and plucked or strummed strings. Voice is a primary instrument, as well.

3. Each style is rendered using a combination of techniques in instrumentation and arrangement that define the style.
4. Each style has its established place in the fascinating and ever-expanding practice of music worldwide.

Music is heard in every country, culture, and community. But what is music? Music that makes sense and is pleasing to one person might sound alien, meaningless, and annoying to another.

In essence, music is the art of sound. It is the art form that uses voices or instrumental sounds, often in various combinations, to express emotions, create audible beauty, or convey messages. Music is a sequence of sounds that people have arranged in a way that pleases or makes sense to them. It can be as simple as an individual tapping out a rhythmic beat on a hollow stick or drum to accompany dancing. It may be a mother humming a nursery lullaby or singing a children's song, or a wandering minstrel singing ballads that tell stories.

On the other hand, it can be as complex as a choral and orchestral score that requires many voices or instruments and takes several hours to perform. It may consist of experiments with abstract electronic sounds. Music recordings today might consist of hundreds of vocal and instrumental tracks, recorded at different times and in far-flung studios, then mixed together.

It is a protean art form, meaning it encompasses a great variety of forms and meanings. Music easily can accompany words in a song or physical movements in a dance. It also can be relevant and interesting by itself.

Throughout history, music has been an important accompaniment to other art forms, most notably drama, and to traditional rituals. In past centuries, music, theatre, acrobatics, magic, and sporting contests provided live entertainment for royalty as well as for the masses. Popular culture has exploited the possibilities. Today, music dominates the arts. It is broadcast to the farthest corners of the globe by means of radio, film, television, musical theatre, and the Internet. Live performances, meanwhile, have never ceased to entertain, inform, and impact contemporary society.

Music can convey human emotions so profoundly that listeners are compelled to cry or laugh. Even without lyrics, music can make listeners feel happy, sad, excited, motivated, or calm. The uses of music in psychotherapy, geriatrics, and advertising testify to its power to affect human behaviour.

Publications and recordings effectively have internationalized music. An Internet search quickly can bring examples of the music of practically any country to the ears of listeners in any other country. This has broadened worldwide familiarity with both significant music and trivial, short-lived genres.

Beyond all this, the teaching of music in primary and secondary schools has attained virtually worldwide acceptance. Music undeniably is an important part of the world in which all cultures coexist. That underscores the importance of music education.

Music, in one style or another, is an expression found in all human societies. It has been enjoyed and used in rituals and ceremonies for thousands of years. Some music goes along with religious observances. Other music is part of everyday life. In many cultures, ancient music has been handed down through the generations and basically preserved as it originally was performed, and it continues to be performed. This is called traditional or folk music.

Most cultures perform distinct styles of music. In Western civilization, classical music is a formal and artistic form that developed in Europe over hundreds of years. Orchestras, choirs, and chamber ensembles (small groups of musicians) often perform classical music. Opera is a type of classical music that features dramatic singing. Other examples of classical music forms include the symphony, a lengthy composition for a full orchestra, and the concerto, in which a solo instrument is featured with an ensemble. Music that is sung without instrumental accompaniment is called *a capella*.

When large numbers of people enjoy a type of music, it is called *popular music*. Generally, popular music is shorter and simpler than classical music. People often buy recordings of popular music or listen to it on the radio or through the computer.

Basic styles of popular music include rock, blues, country, jazz, rap, and hip-hop. Since the 1980s, innovative performers have created unique new styles. Variations include alternative rock, alternative folk, and indie (independent) pop. Many listeners, young and old, have become intrigued with what is called *world music*. It encompasses sounds from many countries and cultures, sometimes experimentally fused.

Music is played on four kinds of instruments: stringed, wind, percussion, and keyboard. Stringed instruments include the violin and mandolin families, harps, and guitars. Violins and similar instruments are played by drawing the fibres—usually made of synthetics—of a bow across a string, to produce a tone. Harps and mandolins are plucked with the fingers or with plastic or metal picks. Guitars are either plucked or strummed. Various other stringed instruments are banjos, acoustic or electric basses, and traditional instruments of other cultures such as the sitar (India) and ukulele (Hawaii).

Wind instruments produce sound when air is passed through an opening. They include woodwinds such as flutes and brass horns such as trumpets. (In symphony orchestras, the woodwinds and brass instruments are seated in separate sections.) Wind instruments also include harmonicas, accordions, tin whistles, fifes, clarinets, oboes, and trombones. A child's kazoo is a simple wind instrument.

Percussion instruments are played by striking or shaking. Skin or synthetic heads of drums are drawn tightly across open cylinders; they are struck with the hands or wooden sticks. Maracas are examples of rattling percussion instruments; they are made of small, dried, enclosed gourds filled with seeds or pebbles, which sound when shaken. Other percussion instruments include wood blocks, metal triangles, tambourines, castanets, bagpipes, and clappers.

Keyboard instruments include pianos, organs, and electronic instruments that are played by pressing keys, buttons, or levers. Music is made when the pressed keys strike a sounding board or mechanism. Harpsichords were among the earliest keyboard instruments. Different types of synthesizers are popular electronic keyboards.

Within the four basic instrument groups, thousands of instrument definitions exist. The violin, for example, has a very deep and wide ancestry spanning several continents over many centuries. In Western culture, the violin family consists of the violin, viola, cello, and double base. Similar bowed instruments, though, are found in various cultures. Examples are the *rebab*, common in the Middle East, and the *orutu* in Kenya. Similarly, there are different types of banjos, mainly the four-string (jazz) and five-string (bluegrass) variations; the African kora bears a striking resemblance. Brass instruments include—besides the most common trumpet, trombone, and tuba—the cornet, euphonium, flugelhorn, and others.

Technique refers to the ways in which music is composed, arranged, and performed. Composing and arranging technique is characterized by the use of melody, harmony, rhythm, counterpoint, dynamics, instrumentation, and other elements as well as overall thematic development.

Fundamental techniques in instrumentation are bowing (violin), plucking (lute and guitar), beating (drums), and blowing (wind instruments). There are many subtleties: sustained notes, ornamental notes, accented rhythms, etc. New techniques have evolved in electronic music. Vocal techniques involve characteristics such as resonation, articulation, breath and tone control, and expression.

For musicians, learning to play an instrument, sing, or compose is only the beginning. Mastering techniques is a lifelong endeavour. African *djembe* drummers train for years before they are considered master drummers, or *djembefolas*. It took Ludwig van Beethoven almost four years to complete his *Symphony No. 5*; many of the musicians who perform it have applied themselves to years of full-time commitment, determined to perfect their talent.

Music: Techniques, Styles, Instruments, and Practice guides readers through the fundamental elements of music: rhythm, melody, harmony, and form. Not all four components are required in every piece of music.

Rhythm involves time—the duration of musical sounds. Tempo, the speed at which a piece is played, is sometimes associated with rhythm. Essential to rhythm are pulsation, or a steady beat, metre, and accent. When beats are combined in groups of two, three, or more to a measure, the result is called metre. Patterns of stress—strong and weak accents—are repeated over and over, as in the waltz rhythm: ONE-two-three, ONE-two-three.

Melody involves pitch, or the relative highness or lowness of tone. When pitches are musically organized, they are referred to as scales. Some types of music consist mostly of melody. Other types may be based on a motif, or recurring succession of notes—for example, the famous notes at the beginning of Beethoven's *Symphony No. 5.* When the melody in a longer composition is repeated in various forms, this basic tune is said to constitute its theme, or subject.

The building of chords—tones played together—derived from the scale on which the music is based is called harmony. It also involves the order in which successions of chords accompany a melody. An example of the effective use of harmony is the second movement of Beethoven's *Symphony No. 7.* The initial melody is a monotone tune (one with almost no variation), but the shifting harmony adds colour, tension, and release to the composition.

Musical form results from the way in which rhythm, melody, and harmony are put together. Good music has unity to satisfy a listener's ear and variety to maintain interest. One of the simplest musical forms is produced by varying and repeating the melody. For example, "Twinkle, Twinkle, Little Star" states a tune, varies it, then restates it.

Music: Techniques, Styles, Instruments, and Practice also explains musical notation, composition, performance, and expression, the multitude of instruments musicians use, and other components of the art form. It provides a special focus on the styles and genres of music in Western cultures.

CHAPTER ONE

MUSIC NOTATION, SOUND, AND THE STRUCTURE OF MUSIC

All music includes basic elements, or parts. The main elements of music are rhythm, melody, harmony, and form.

Rhythm describes the length of musical sounds. The most important part of rhythm is the pulse, or beat. When you tap your foot to a song you like, you are tapping out the beat. The speed of the beats is called the tempo. The pattern of the beats is called the metre. Drums help other instruments and voices keep the rhythm in many songs.

Melody is a series of different tones, or sounds, in a piece of music. The notes are played or sung one after another to make up a song. The tones in a melody may be low or high. The highness or lowness of a tone is called its pitch. Musicians describe different tones with the letters A, B, C, D, E, F, and G.

Harmony takes place when people play or sing more than one tone at the same time. Groups of tones played together are called chords. Harmony also describes the way chords go along with a melody.

Form is the way that people put rhythm, melody, and harmony together. There are many different types of musical forms. Repeating a short melody is one of the simplest forms. For example, in the song "Mary Had a Little Lamb," each verse repeats the same melody. A symphony is a more complex form. In a symphony, different groups of instruments may play different melodies at the same time or a series of harmonies. The rhythm may also change—for example, the tempo may be fast or slow at different points in the symphony.

Some musicians make up music as they perform. Others sing songs or play pieces that someone else created. Musicians have developed a system for writing down music so that others can play it again. They use certain symbols, called notes, to indicate the tones to be played or sung. The arrangement of the notes

A musician writes musical notes on a sheet while she sits at a piano. There are some musicians who write music as they perform.

shows the order in which the tones should be played. Other numbers and symbols show how fast to play each note. These numbers and symbols are known as music notation.

MUSIC NOTATION

To understand music notation and structure, it is necessary for a person to know something about sound in general. A sound is produced by the vibration of an object. If the vibration is irregular, the result is noise. If the vibration is regular, the result is a musical sound, or tone. Not until the late 19th century was it known that electric impulses could produce sounds from an instrument. Until this discovery—the forerunner of today's electronic music—the human performer was indispensable in the creation of musical sounds.

Tones have a definite pitch, which may be high, low, or in the middle range, depending upon the rate at which vibration takes place. Slow vibration creates low tones; fast vibration, high tones.

The rudiments of music are best described in terms of the piano, which has 88 pitches, or tones. These tones are produced by striking each of the 88 black and white piano keys. Only the first seven letters of the alphabet are needed to name the white keys. The black keys represent sharps and flats. Starting at the left of the keyboard—the end with the lowest tone—the first white key is A, the second is B, and so on through G. At the eighth key, and at every eighth key thereafter, the designations begin again at A. The distance between any piano key and the nearest key of the same name is an octave.

Each piano key has a vibration rate that is exactly twice as great as that of the one an octave below it. Thus, the first C's rate is 32 times a second, the second C's rate is 64, and so on up the piano keyboard. For the eighth C—the highest tone on the piano—the frequency rate is more than 4,000 cycles per second.

MUSICAL SOUND IN WESTERN MUSIC TRADITIONS

Musical sound is defined as any tone with characteristics such as controlled pitch and timbre. The sounds are produced by instruments in which the periodic vibrations can be controlled by the performer.

That some sounds are intrinsically musical, while others are not, is an oversimplification. From the tinkle of a bell to the slam of a door, any sound is a potential ingredient for the kinds of sound organization called music. The choices of sounds for music making have been severely limited in all places and periods by a diversity of physical, aesthetic, and cultural considerations.

The fundamental distinction usually made has been between tone and noise, a distinction best clarified by referring to the physical characteristics of sound. Tone differs from noise mainly in that it possesses features that enable it to be regarded as autonomous. Noises are most readily identified, not by their character but by their sources; e.g., the noise of the dripping faucet, the grating chalk, or the squeaking gate. Although tones too are commonly linked with their sources (violin tone, flute tone, etc.), they more readily achieve autonomy because they possess controlled pitch, loudness, timbre, and duration, attributes that make them amenable to musical organization. Instruments that yield musical sounds, or tones, are those that produce periodic vibrations. Their periodicity is their controllable (i.e., musical) basis.

The strings of the violin, the lips of the trumpet player, the reed of a saxophone, and the wooden slabs of a xylophone are all, in their unique ways, producers of periodic vibrations. The pitch, or high-low aspect, created by each of these vibrating bodies is most directly a product of vibrational frequency. Timbre (tone colour) is a product of the total complement of simultaneous motions enacted by any medium during its vibration. Loudness is a product of the intensity of that motion. Duration is the length of time that a tone persists.

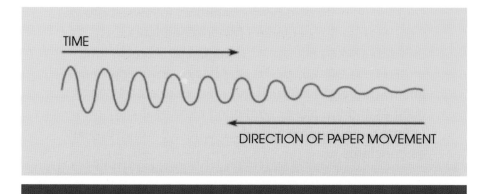

TIME

DIRECTION OF PAPER MOVEMENT

This illustration is a visual representation of a reed's vibration.

Each of these attributes is revealed in the wave form of a tone. The pattern may be visualized as an elastic reed—like that of a clarinet—fixed at one end, moving like a pendulum in a to-and-fro pattern when set into motion. Clearly, this reed's motion will be in proportion to the applied force. Its arc of movement will be lesser or greater depending upon the degree of pressure used to set it into motion. Once moving, it will oscillate until friction and its own inertia cause it to return to its original state of rest. As it moves through its arc the reed passes through a periodic number of cycles per time unit, although its speed is not constant. With these conditions prevailing, its motion through time could be charted by placing a carbon stylus on its moving head, then pulling a strip of paper beneath it at a uniform rate. The reed's displacement to-and-fro diminishes in a smooth fashion as time passes (decreasing intensity). Each cycle of its arc is equally spaced (uniform frequency). Each period of the motion forms the same arc pattern (uniform wave content). If this vibratory motion were audible, it could be described as follows: it grows weaker from the beginning (diminishing loudness) until it becomes inaudible; it remains at a stable level of highness (steady pitch); and it is of unvarying tonal quality (uniform timbre). If the reed were a part of a clarinet and the player continued blowing it with unvaried pressure, loudness, pitch, and timbre would appear as constants.

TONE

Most musical tones differ from the demonstration tone (above) in that they consist of more than a single wave form. Any material undergoing vibratory motion imposes its own characteristic oscillations on the fundamental vibration. The reed probably would vibrate in parts as well as a whole, thus creating partial wave forms in addition to the fundamental wave form. These partials are not fortuitous. They bear

2 : 1 = OCTAVE
3 : 2 = FIFTH
4 : 3 = FOURTH
5 : 4 = THIRD
8 : 7 = SECOND

FUNDAMENTAL PITCH

ACTUAL PITCH SLIGHTLY LOWER THAN STANDARD NOTATION SHOWS.

harmonic relationships to the fundamental motion that are expressible as frequency ratios of 1:2, 3:4, etc. This means that the reed (or string or air column as well) is vibrating in halves and thirds and fourths as well as a whole. Another way of expressing this is that half the body is vibrating at a frequency twice as great as the whole; a third is vibrating at a frequency three times greater; etc.

These numerical relationships also are expressible by pitch relationships as the harmonic, or overtone, series, which is merely a representation of numerical ratios in terms of pitch equivalents. Depending upon its shape and substance, a vibrating mass performs motions that are the equivalents of these partial vibrations, whether it is the mass of a string, reed, woodblock, or air column. This means that most tones are composites: they consist of partial vibrations of the vibrating body as well as the vibrations of the whole mass. Although one can develop the acuity required to hear some of these overtones within a musical tone, the ear normally ignores them as separate parts, recognizing only a more or less rich tone quality within the fundamental pitch.

Although pure tones, or tones lacking other than a fundamental frequency, sometimes occur in music, most musical tones are composites. A typical violin tone is relatively rich in overtones while a flute tone sometimes approaches a pure tone. What the listener recognizes as "a violin tone" or "a trumpet tone" also is a product of the noise content that accompanies the articulation of any sound on the particular instrument. The friction of the bow as it is set into motion across the string, the eddies of air pressure within a horn's mouthpiece, or the hammer's impact on a piano string all add an extra dimension, a significant "noise factor," to any manually produced tone. After articulation, however, it is the presence or absence of overtones and their relative intensities that determine the timbre of any tone. The violin and flute tones are distinguishable because their articulatory "noises" are quite different and their overtone contents are dissimilar, even when they produce the same pitch.

Musical tones of determined harmonic content can be produced by electronic vacuum tubes or transistors as well as by traditional manual instruments. Some electronic organs, for example, use single vacuum tubes whose frequency output can be varied through control of an adjustable transformer. Through ingenious mixing circuits a compound tone consisting of any predetermined overtone content can be produced, thereby imitating the sound of any traditional instrument. Composers of electronic music have utilized this capability to synthesize tones quite different from any available on traditional instruments, as well as tones similar to natural sounds. Electronic computers are capable of complete imitation of such sounds; the tone is broken down into its component parts, then synthesized through an auditory output circuit.

MOVEMENT

Once an audible oscillation is produced by a vibrating body, it moves away from its source as a spherical pressure wave. Its rate of passage through any medium is determined by the medium's density and elasticity; the denser the medium, the slower the transmission; the greater the elasticity, the faster. In air at around 60° F, sound moves at approximately 1,120 feet per second, the rate increasing by 1.1 feet per second per degree of rise in temperature.

Sound waves move as a succession of compressions through the air. The wavelength is determined by frequency; the higher the pitch, the shorter the wavelength. A pitch of 263 cycles per second (middle C of the piano) is borne as a wavelength of around 4.3 feet (speed of sound ÷ frequency = wavelength).

By the time a wave has moved some distance, it has changed in some of its characteristics. The journey has robbed it of intensity, which is inversely proportional to the square of the distance. Its timbre has been altered slightly by objects within its path that disrupted an equitable distribution of frequencies, particularly the high-frequency waves, which, unlike the low, move in relatively straight paths from their sources.

The area within which a sound occurs can have considerable effect upon what is heard. Just as a string or reed or air column has a natural resonance period (or rate of vibration), any enclosure—whether an audio speaker cabinet or the nave of a cathedral—imposes its resonance characteristics on a sound wave within it. Any tone that approximates in frequency the characteristic resonance period of an enclosure will be reinforced through the sympathetic response, or natural resonance, of the air within the enclosure. This means that tones of frequencies differing from the resonance of the enclosure will be less intense than those that agree, thereby creating an inequity of sound intensities.

Fortunately, most rooms where music is performed are large enough (wall lengths greater than about 30 feet) so that their natural resonance periods are too slow to fall within the range of pitches of the lowest musical tones (usually no lower than 27 cycles per second, although some organs have pipes that extend to 15 cycles per second). Smaller rooms can produce disturbing sympathetic resonance unless obstructions or absorbent materials are added to minimize that effect.

In addition to resonance, any enclosure possesses a reverberation period, a unit of time measured from the instant a sound fills the enclosure (steady state) until that sound has decayed to one-millionth of its initial intensity. Anyone who has spoken or clapped his hands inside a large, empty room has experienced prolonged reverberation. There are two reasons for such protracted reverberation: first, the space between the surfaces of the enclosure is so great that reflected sound waves travel extended distances before decaying; and, second, the absence of highly absorbent materials precludes appreciable loss of intensity of the wave during its movement.

The reverberation period is a crucial factor in rooms where sounds must be heard with considerable fidelity. If the period is too long in a room where speech must be understood, spoken syllables will blend into each other and the words will be mumbled confusion. If, on the other hand, the reverberation period is too brief in a room where human "presence" and music each contribute to the acoustics, only a "cold" and "dull" feeling will persist, because no reverberative support of the prevailing sounds can be provided by the enclosure itself.

Although all sound waves, regardless of their pitch, travel at the same rate of speed through a particular medium, low tones mushroom out in a broad trajectory while high tones move in straight paths. For this reason listeners in any room should be within a direct path of sound propagation. Seats far to the side at the front of an auditorium offer occupants a potentially distorted version of sound from its source. Thus the high-frequency speakers (tweeters) in good audio reproduction systems are angled toward the sides of the room, ensuring wider coverage for high-frequency components of all sounds.

Sites of musical performance in the open demand quite different acoustical arrangements, of course, since sound reflection from ceilings and walls cannot occur and reverberation cannot provide the desirable support that would be available within a room. A reflective shell placed behind the sound source can provide a boost in transmission of sounds toward listeners. Such a reflector must be designed so that relatively uniform wave propagation will reach all locations where listening will occur. The shell form serves that purpose admirably since its curved shape avoids the right angles that might set up continuous reflections, or echoing. Furthermore, sound waves are reflected more uniformly over a wide area than with any other shape, diffusing them equally over the path of propagations. (The needs here are similar to those of the photographer who wishes to flood a scene uniformly with flat light rather than focus with a spotlight on a small area.)

PITCH AND TIMBRE

Just as various denominations of coins combine to form the larger units of a monetary system, so musical tones combine to form larger units of musical experience. Although pitch, loudness, duration, and timbre act as four-fold coordinates in the structuring of these units, pitch has been favoured as the dominating attribute by most Western theorists. The history of music theory has to a great degree consisted of a commentary on the ways pitches are combined to make musical patterns, leaving loudness and timbre more as the "understood" parameters of the musical palette.

Music terminology, for example, recognizes loudness in music in terms of an eight-level continuum of nuances from "extremely soft" (ppp, or *pianississimo*) to "extremely loud" (fff or *fortississimo*). (The musical dominance of Italy from the late 16th to the 18th century—when these Italian terms first were applied—explains their retention today.)

The timbres of music enjoy an even less explicit and formalized ranking; other than the vague classifications "shrill," "mellow," "full," and so on, there is no standard taxonomy of tone quality. Musicians for the most part are content to denote a particular timbre by the name of the instrument that produced it.

Pitch is another matter. A highly developed musical culture demands a precise standardization of pitch, and Western theory has been occupied with this task from as early as Aristoxenus (4th century BCE). Especially since the Renaissance, when instruments emerged as the principal vehicles of the musical impulse, problems of pitch location (tuning) and representation (notation) have challenged the practicing musician. When at least two instrumentalists sit down to play a duet, there must be some agreement about pitch, or only frustration will result. Although the standardization of the pitch name a′ (within the middle of the piano keyboard) at 440 cycles per second has been adopted by most of the professional music world, there was a day—even during the mid-18th century of Bach—when pitch uniformity was unknown.

Human perception of pitch is confined within a span of roughly 15 to 18,000 cycles per second. This upper limit varies with the age and ear structure of the individual, the upper limit normally attenuating with advancing age. The pitch spectrum is divided into octaves, a name derived from the scale theories of earlier times when only eight (Latin *octo*) notes within this breadth were codified. Today the octave is considered in Western music to define the boundaries for the pitches of the chromatic scale. The piano keyboard is a useful visual representation of this 12-unit division of the octave. Beginning on any key, there are 12 different keys (and thus 12 different pitches), counting the beginning key, before a key occupying the same position in the pattern recurs.

One must keep in mind that the chromatic scale, within the various octave registers of man's hearing, is merely a conventional standard of pitch tuning. Performers like singers, trombone and string players, who can alter the pitches they produce, frequently make use of pitches that do not correspond precisely to this set of norms. The music of many non-Western cultures also utilizes distinct divisions of the octave. Furthermore, some contemporary music makes use of pitch placements that divide the octave into units smaller than the half step. This music, called microtonal, has not become standard fare in Western cultures, in spite of its advocates (Alois Hába, Julian Carillo, Karlheinz Stockhausen) and even its special instruments that provide a means for consistent performance.

Western music history is dotted with systems formulated for the precise tuning of pitches within the octave. From a modern viewpoint all suffer from one of two mutually exclusive faults: either they lack relationships (intervals) of uniform size, or they are incapable of providing chords that are acceptable to the ear. Pythagorean tuning provides uniformity but not the chords. Just tuning, based on the simpler ratios of the overtone series, provides the chords but suffers from inequality of intervals. Meantone tuning provides equal intervals but gives rise to several objectionable chords, even in simple music. All three of these systems fail to provide the pitch wherewithal for the 12 musical keys found in the standard repertoire.

The compromise tuning system most widely accepted since the mid-19th century is called "equal temperament." Based on the division of the octave into 12 equal half steps, or semitones, this method provides precisely equal intervals and a full set of chords that, although not as euphonious as those of the overtone series, are not offensive to the listener.

The semitone is the smallest acknowledged interval of the Western pitch system. The sizes of all remaining intervals can be calculated by determining how many semitones each contains. The names of these intervals are derived from musical notation through a simple counting of lines and spaces of the staff (see illustration on page 15). Just as the

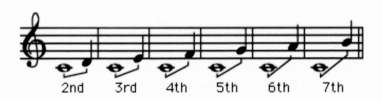

GENERIC NAMES OF PITCH INTERVALS.

overtone content of a single tone determines timbre, the relationship of the constituent pitches of an interval determines its quality, or sonance. There is a long history of speculations in this area, but the subjectivity of the data indicates that little verifiable fact can be sorted from it.

Until the 20th century, music theorists were prone to concoct tables that showed an "objective" classification of intervals into the two opposing camps of consonant and dissonant. But only the person who utters these terms can know with assurance what he means by them, although many attempts have been made to link consonant with pleasant, smooth, stable, beautiful and dissonant with unpleasant, grating, unstable, and ugly. These adjectives may be reasonably meaningful in musical contexts, but difficulty arises if one attempts to pin a singular evaluation on a particular interval per se.

Theorists have noted that the character of an interval is altered considerably by the sounds that surround it. Thus the naked interval that sounds "grating," "unstable," and lacking in fusion might within a particular context create an altogether different effect, and vice versa.

Recognition of the power of context in shaping a response to the individual pitch interval has led some music theorists to think more in terms of a continuum of sonance that extends from more consonant to more dissonant, tearing down the artificial fence once presumed to separate the two in experience.

The explanation of consonance and dissonance offered by Hermann von Helmholtz in *On the Sensations of Tone* (1863) is perhaps as helpful as any. An initial theory was based on the notion that dissonance is a product of beats, which result from simultaneous tones or their upper overtones of slightly differing frequencies. Another explanation, offered later by Helmholtz, held that two tones are consonant if they have one or more overtones (excluding the seventh and ninth) in common (see illustration).

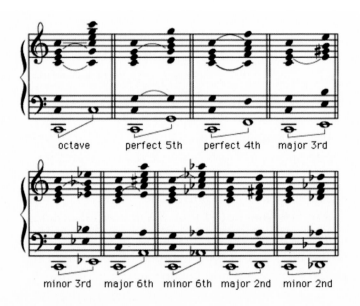

COMMON OVERTONES (INCOMPLETE SERIES, EXCLUDING THE SEVENTH) AT VARIOUS PITCH INTERVALS.

Music in which a high degree of dissonance occurs has rekindled interest in this old problem of psychoacoustics. The German composer Paul Hindemith (1895–1963) provided one explanation of harmonic tension and relaxation that depends upon the intervals found within chords. According to his view a chord is more dissonant than another if it contains a greater number of intervals that, as separate entities, are dissonant. Although Hindemith's reasoning and conclusions have not been widely accepted, the absence of any more convincing explanation and classification often leads musicians to use his ideas implicitly.

Although the complete pitch spectrum can be tuned in a way that provides 12 pitches per octave (as the chromatic scale), pitch organization in music usually is discussed in terms of less inclusive kinds of scale patterns. The most important scales in traditional Western theory are seventone (heptatonic), which, like the chromatic, operate within the octave. These scales are different from one another only in the intervals formed by their constituent pitches. The major scale, for instance, consists of seven pitches arranged in the intervallic order: tone–tone–semitone–tone–tone–tone–semitone.

Called major because of the large (or major) third that separates the first and third pitches, this scale differs from the minor scale mainly in that the latter contains a small (or minor) third in this location. Since three variants of the minor scale are recognized in the music of the Western repertoire, it is important to note that they share this small interval between their first and third pitches.

Major and minor scales formed the primary pitch ingredients of music written between 1650 and 1900, although this is a sweeping generalization for which exceptions are not rare. Other scales, called modes, possess greater representational power for music of earlier times and for much of the repertoire of Western folk music. These too are heptatonic patterns, their uniqueness produced solely by the differing pitch relationships formed by their members. Each of the modes can most easily be reproduced by playing successive white keys at the piano.

The modes and the major and minor scales best represent the pitch structure of Western music, though they do not utilize the total complement of 12 chromatic pitches per octave. They are abstractions that are meaningful for tonal music; i.e., music in which a particular pitch acts as a focal point of perception, establishing a sense of repose or tonality to which the remaining six pitches relate. Major and minor scale tonality was basic to Western music until it began to disintegrate in the art music of the late 19th century. It was replaced in part by the methods of Arnold Schoenberg (1874–1951), which used all 12 notes as basic material. Since that revolution of the early 1920s, the raw pitch materials of Western music have frequently been drawn from the complete chromatic potential. By contrast, the music of several Eastern cultures, a number of children's songs, and occasional Western folk songs incorporate pitch materials best classified as *pentatonic* (a five-pitch scale).

SOUND PRODUCTION OF MUSICAL INSTRUMENTS

Excluding electronic tone synthesizers, which employ vacuum tubes or transistors to produce tones, musical instruments can be classified within three groups: (1) chordophones, or strings; (2) aerophones, or winds; and (3) idiophones and membranophones, nearly all of which are percussion instruments. Each category is further divisible into groups according to the way the vibrating medium is set into motion.

Three means of eliciting sounds determine three categories within the family of chordophones. They are bowing, plucking, and striking. Most common of the first category are the violin, viola, violoncello, and double bass of the orchestra, all of which use a horsehair bow for setting their strings into motion. Essentially a resonant box bearing strings of four different fundamental frequencies, members of this group have not changed appreciably in construction since the 17th century, except for the 20th-century advent of the electrified bass, which is in fact a close cousin of the amplified guitar.

Violins and the larger members of its group are sounded by plucking (pizzicato) on occasion, which provides a brittle tone of extremely brief duration. The harp is the best known orchestral instrument whose tone depends upon the noise components added by plucking. Other plucked instruments are the guitar, banjo, mandolin, ukelele, zither, lyre, lute, and the harpsichord. The latter differs from the piano in that its strings are actuated by the plucking action of a tiny plectrum.

The piano is most notable of the struck stringed instruments, employing a hammer mechanism linked with the keyboard for producing its wide range of sounds. Other instruments of this group are the clavichord and the dulcimer.

For all chordophones pitch is proportional to string tension and inversely proportional to length, thickness, and density. Since string length is the most readily altered of these factors, all chordophones provide a means for altering the resonating length of strings (as with the violin and guitar) or a set of many string lengths and masses (as with the piano and harp) for producing a variety of pitches.

This category covers everything from the piccolo to the pipe organ and is best understood by consistent reference to the nature of the air column employed in the various types of instruments, as well as the way this air column is set into motion.

Brass instruments consist of a long tube whose cross section is proportionately small. Coupled with a mouthpiece that, in response to vibrations of the performer's lips, helps to create eddies of air pressure that set an enclosed air column into motion, these instruments produce a range of pitches corresponding to the overtone series. The bugle is a primitive kind of brass instrument in that it is limited to only one overtone series, while the modern trumpet, cornet, French horn, trombone, tuba, flügelhorn, and various kinds of euphoniums utilize valves or a slide to lengthen the air column and thus provide up to seven different overtone series. Pitch on these instruments is primarily a function of tube length, the wavelength of the instrument's fundamental pitch equal to twice the length of the tube, plus a so-called end correction that accommodates variations of bore. Timbre is a product of mouthpiece shape, bore (whether cylindrical or conical), and material, aside from the important role performed by the player himself in obtaining desired overtones.

Woodwinds prior to the 20th century were made for the most part of wood. Flutes and clarinets are classified in this group only because of this heritage, while the saxophones, always built of metal, share only the reed mouthpiece and similar fingering technique with the clarinet. All are, nonetheless, called woodwinds, and they consist of an air column set into motion by one of two means: (1) through high pressure eddies produced by the wind of the performer blown directly into the instrument (as with a recorder or whistle) or over it (as with the flute and piccolo), or (2) by means of a vibrating reed that is set into motion by air pressure from the performer. The clarinets and saxophones utilize a single reed fixed at one end, while the oboe, English horn, and bassoon use two thin reeds that are connected laterally and vibrate jointly. For all of these instruments, either keys or the fingers of the performer directly open holes, with the effect of shortening the enclosed air column of the instrument and thereby producing higher fundamental pitches. Through overblowing and various fingering procedures, the overtone series provides the wealth of pitches available on these instruments.

Free reed instruments utilize a single, freely vibrating reed, different in nature from that of a woodwind. The category includes the accordion, harmonica, and harmonium and their relatives. In these instruments the reed vibrates, causing periodic vibrations in the air; but the reed's size, rather than the air enclosed by the instrument, determines the pitch.

Pipe organs are of the aerophone (wind) category, too, although their keyboard mechanism and literature link them closely with the piano and harpsichord. Like a grand synthesis of woodwinds and brasses, organs produce their tones by means of tuned air columns that are formed with pipes of varied length, cross section, and shape (called flue pipes) or by means of a vibrating brass reed actuated by forced air (called reed pipes). Flue pipes range in length from under an inch to 32 feet.

Idiophones are instruments whose bodies vibrate to produce sound. The class contains most of the pitched percussion instruments. These include instruments made of wood or other organic material, such as xylophones. They also include pitched percussion instruments that are struck or plucked and are made of metal or other inorganic material (triangle, glockenspiel, vibraphone, celesta, tubular bell, gong, steel drum, cymbal, glass harmonica, etc.). Idiophones without pitch consist of such instruments as the percussion board, castanets, and rattles, all of which are made of wood or other organic material and are struck, scraped, rubbed, brushed, or shaken.

Membranophones produce sound by a vibrating membrane. The group consists most notably of the timpani, or kettledrums, which can be tuned by increasing or decreasing the tension of the membranes that form the heads of the enclosed cavities. Other membranophones consist of drums without fixed pitch, such as side drums, bongos, and various non-Western types of fixed and indefinite pitch. Tone quality and character are the result of the player's skill in controlling intensity and overtone character of the sound.

HOW MUSIC IS WRITTEN

Just as language is recorded with a set of letters that represent spoken sounds, music is recorded with a set of symbols that represent musical sounds. This system of symbols, called notation, tells musicians the pitch and the duration of each sound they are to play. The rhythm, the tempo, and the dynamics (softness or loudness) of the music to be played are indicated by other symbols.

THE NOTATION OF PITCH

Musical tones are represented on paper by notes placed on a staff consisting of five horizontal lines and the four intervening spaces. The higher the tone is in pitch, the higher its place on the staff.

STAFFS AND CLEFS

Notes for higher-pitched tones appear on the treble staff, which is marked with a treble, or G, clef sign. The sign has a curl around the next to the bottom line of the staff. This is the line above middle C on which G is written.

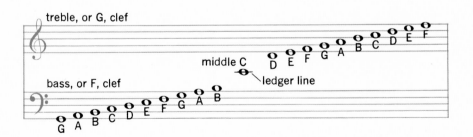

TREBLE CLEF AND BASS CLEF

Other notes are located in relation to the G line, those that are above it moving upward on the staff and those below it downward. The stems of notes go toward the third, or B, line; for B, the stem usually goes downward.

Notes indicating lower pitches are placed on the bass staff, marked by a bass, or F, clef sign. The two dots of the clef enclose the staff line on which F below middle C is written.

Short ledger lines are used for notes that are too high or too low to appear on the five lines of a staff. For notes that require a great many ledger lines, the following sign is often substituted:

8 va ～

When this notation appears over a group of notes, it indicates that they are to be played an octave higher than they are written. Placed under a group of notes, the sign indicates that the notes are to be played an octave lower than written.

Most music is written on the treble and bass staffs. Music for the viola and some other instruments, however, is written on a staff marked with a C clef:

𝄡

The staff line that passes between the two curves of the C clef is fixed as middle C. In music for the piano, the treble and bass staffs are joined together by a line or a bracket.

SHARPS AND FLATS

On the piano the distance from a white key to the nearest black key is a half step, or semitone. (The instances in which semitones occur between white keys are E-F and B-C.) When a tone is to be raised a half step, a sharp (

#

) sign is used. The black key just above D is D

#

. When this tone is called for, the sharp is written on the staff to the left of the D note. When a tone is to be lowered a half step, a flat (

♭

) sign is used. The black key just below D is D

♭

, and the flat is written on the staff to the left of the D. If the original tone is to be played shortly after a sharp or flat sign appeared with it, a natural (

♮

) sign is used. These notations—

#

,

♭

, and

♮

—appearing alongside a note within a piece are called accidentals.

Two other accidental signs are the double sharp (

𝕏 or ✳

) and the double flat (

♭♭

). The double sharp indicates a note one whole step (two half steps) above the original note. The double flat indicates a note one whole step below the original note. A natural sign can be used to cancel a double sharp or flat.

DURATION AND RHYTHM

The longest note is the whole note. Next is the half note, then the quarter note, and so on, up to the sixty-fourth note. Notes with shorter values than the quarter note have flags, or "tails," on their stems. The whole note has the same time value as—or equals—two half notes. A whole note also equals 4 quarter notes, 8 eighth notes, and so on, up to 64 sixty-fourth notes. When two or more eighth notes or shorter notes follow each other, they are often joined.

eighth notes   sixteenth notes   thirty-second notes   sixty-fourth notes

A dot after a note increases its duration by one half. Thus a quarter note followed by a dot has a duration of one quarter note plus one eighth note. Duration is also increased by the tie—a curved line connecting a note and the repetition of it. The tie makes the total duration of a note equal to that of the notes connected. When there is to be no sound, a rest is used. Rests have the same time value as notes of the same duration, ranging from a whole rest to a sixty-fourth rest.

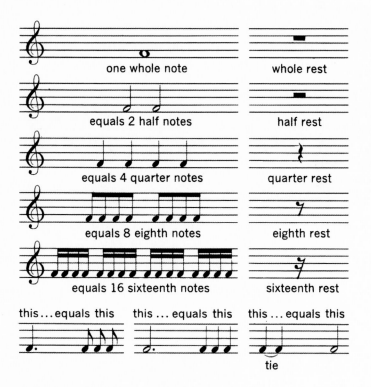

MUSICAL NOTES AND RESTS

As explained earlier, one aspect of rhythm is metre—the recurring pattern of strong and weak beats. The metre is indicated at the beginning of written music by a time signature. This consists of two numerals, one over the other. The upper numeral tells how many beats there are to the measure; the lower numeral shows the kind of note that receives one beat. A time signature of

$$\frac{2}{4},$$

for example, means that there are two beats to each measure and that a quarter note receives one beat. The other notes receive beats or fractions of beats according to their relative time values. A half note would be given two beats, an eighth note one half beat, and so on.

1 2   1 2   1   2   1 2

TIME SIGNATURE

Some other time signatures are

$$\frac{4}{4}$$

(the most common and often indicated by the sign

𝄴), $\frac{3}{4}$, $\frac{3}{8}$,

and

$$\frac{6}{8}$$

. Less frequently used are

$$\frac{5}{4}$$

and

$$\frac{7}{8}$$

.

Each repetition of the basic metre is indicated by vertical lines on the staff, called bars, that divide the notes into units. Each unit is a measure and usually has the same number of beats.

TEMPO AND DYNAMICS

The tempo may be indicated by a metronome marking—for example,

♩

= 96, which means that the piece is to be played at a rate of 96 quarter notes per minute. By using a metronome, the musician can follow the tempo exactly. This timekeeping device can be adjusted to tick from 40 to 208 times per minute. Each tick marks a beat.

Tempo may also be indicated by descriptive words, which are usually in Italian. Some of the commonest, with their meanings, are: Largo (slow tempo); Moderato and Andante (medium tempo); Allegro,

piano	*p*	soft
pianissimo	*pp*	very soft
forte	*f*	loud
fortissimo	*ff*	very loud
mezzo piano	*mp*	medium soft
mezzo forte	*mf*	medium loud
crescendo	*cresc.* <	gradually louder
diminuendo	*dim.* >	gradually softer

DYNAMIC MARKINGS

Vivace, and Presto (fast tempo); Ritardando (gradually slower); and Accelerando (gradually faster). Italian words and their abbreviations are also used for dynamic markings, indicating degrees of softness or loudness.

THE STRUCTURE OF MUSIC

The foundation of a musical composition is the scale upon which it is based. A scale is a series of tones arranged according to pitch. From the tones of the scale, the composer makes up his melody. The harmony, or chordal arrangement that accompanies the melody, is also based on the scale.

Many kinds of scales are possible. One of the oldest is the pentatonic (5-note) scale. Playing the five black keys between F above middle C and the F an octave above it on the piano gives an idea of how a pentatonic scale sounds. Many old songs, such as "Auld Lang Syne," are based on the pentatonic scale and can be played entirely on the black keys. Most music composed between 1600 and 1900, however, is based upon the 8-note diatonic scale.

MELODY

Melody is the aesthetic product of a given succession of pitches in musical time, implying rhythmically ordered movement from pitch to pitch. Melody in Western music by the late 19th century was considered to be the surface of a group of harmonies. The top tone of a chord became a melody tone; chords were chosen for their colour and sense of direction relative to each other and were spaced so that a desired succession of tones lay on top. Any melody, then, had underlying chords that could be deduced. Thus, a good guitarist, analyzing mentally, can apply chords to a melody.

(CONTINUED ON THE NEXT PAGE)

(CONTINUED FROM THE PREVIOUS PAGE)

But melody is far older than harmony. The single line of melody was highly developed–e.g., in medieval European and Byzantine plainchant, in the melodies of the trouvères and troubadours, and in the ragas and *maqāmāt* (melody types) of Indian and Arab music. Combining several lines of melody at once is polyphony; varying a melody in different ways in simultaneous performance is heterophony; combining melody and chords is homophony.

A melodic line has several characteristics that, taken together, describe it:

1. It has contour, an overall line that rises, falls, arches, undulates, or moves in any other characteristic way. For example, the first line of "My Bonnie Lies Over the Ocean" rises with a leap, then descends more or less stepwise. Melodic motion may be disjunctive, using leaps, or conjunctive, moving by steps; motion helps form the melody's contour.

2. Melody also has range: it occupies a certain space within the spectrum of pitches the human ear can perceive. Some primitive melodies have a range of two notes; the soprano solo in the "Kyrie eleison" of Mozart's *Mass in C Minor* (K. 427) has a range of two octaves.

3. Melody has a scale. In musically sophisticated cultures, scales are formally

recognized as systems of tones from which melody can be built. Melody, however, antedates the concept of scale. Scales may be abstracted from their melodies by listing the tones used in order of pitch. The intervals of a melody's scale contribute to its overall character. When children sing the ditty found throughout Europe, "It's raining, it's pouring" (g–g–e–a–g–e), they sing a melody that uses a scale of three tones; two intervals are used, a wide one (minor third) and a narrow one (major second). The harmonic minor scale of western Europe contains an interval not found in the major scale–an augmented second, as A♭–B–which contributes to the distinctive quality of many minor melodies. African and European melodies sometimes consist of chains of intervals, e.g., of thirds or fourths.

Composers and improvisers draw from a number of melodic resources:

1. A theme is a melody that is not necessarily complete in itself except when designed for a set of variations but is recognizable as a pregnant phrase or clause. A fugue subject is a theme; the expositions and episodes of a sonata are groups of themes.
2. Figures or motives, small fragments of a theme, are grouped into new melodies in

(CONTINUED ON THE NEXT PAGE)

(CONTINUED FROM THE PREVIOUS PAGE)

the "development" of a sonata. In a fugue, they carry on the music when the subject and countersubject are silent.

3. In a sequence, a figure or group of chords is repeated at different levels of pitch.

4. Ornaments, or graces (small melodic devices such as grace notes, appoggiaturas, trills, slides, tremolo, and slight deviations from standard pitch), may be used to embellish a melody. Melodic ornamentation is present in most European music and is essential to Indian, Arabic, Japanese, and much other non-Western music.

Some musical systems have complex formulaic structures called modes or melody types with which melodies are built.

MAJOR AND MINOR SCALES

The 8-note diatonic scale has two variations—the major scale and the minor scale. There are 15 major scales and three types of minor scales.

Starting with middle C and playing all the white piano keys up to the next C produces the diatonic scale of C major. Notice the uneven pattern of whole steps and half steps. There is a half step between the 3rd and 4th tones and between the 7th and 8th tones. All the other tones are a whole step apart.

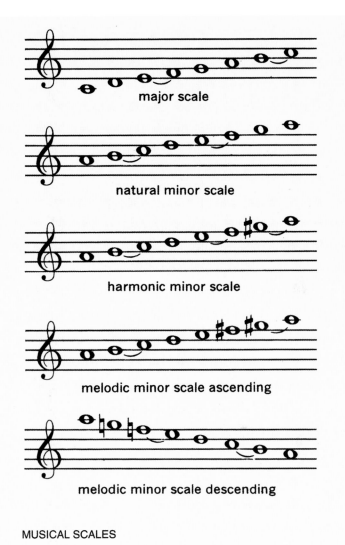

major scale

natural minor scale

harmonic minor scale

melodic minor scale ascending

melodic minor scale descending

MUSICAL SCALES

Each of the 15 major scales has its own relative minor scale—the natural minor scale—which begins on the sixth note of the major scale. The other two forms of the minor scale are the harmonic minor scale and the melodic minor scale.

In the natural minor scale the half steps occur between the 2nd and 3rd and between the 5th and 6th notes of the scale. In the harmonic minor scale the 7th note of the natural minor scale is raised a half step so there are one and one half steps between the 6th and 7th notes and a half step between the 7th and 8th. In the melodic minor scale the 6th and 7th notes of the natural minor are each raised a half step in the ascending scale; the whole and half steps of the descending scale are the same as in the natural minor.

The starting note for either a major or a minor scale is the tonic, or keynote. To preserve the scale pattern of half steps and whole steps, sharps and flats are used. Thus, in the scale of D major, the notes played are: D-E-F

\#

-(half step)-G-A-B-C

\#

—(half step)-D. Rather than write the sharp sign beside F and C throughout the piece, the composer places sharp signs on the F and C lines of the staff at the beginning of the piece. Any note on lines F and C is then to be played as F and C

\#

, and the piece is said to be in the key of D major. Sharps or flats placed on the staff at the beginning of a piece constitute the key signature. Music with no key signature is in the key of C major or A minor.

HARMONY

Harmony results from the construction of chords—three or more different notes sounded at the same time. The note that originates a chord is called the root. In simple harmonic progressions the three most important chords are the tonic (I), the dominant seventh (V7), and the subdominant (IV).

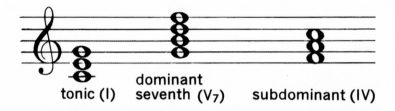

tonic (I)   dominant seventh (V₇)   subdominant (IV)

IMPORTANT CHORDS

A chord is constructed from notes of a scale in intervals of thirds. An interval is the musical distance between two notes of a scale. It is computed by counting the lower note played, the notes between, and the higher note played. From C to E is a third, and from E to G is also a third. This combination of three notes—C-E-G—is a triad and in the key of C major makes up the most frequently used chord, the tonic.

The dominant seventh chord, in the key of C, is built on G, the fifth note of that scale. The chord notes would then be G-B-D-F—F being the 7th note above G. The subdominant chord, in the key of C, is built on the fourth note of the scale, or F. This chord is F-A-C. The tonic and these two chords may serve as the accompaniment to many simple songs.

DIATONIC SCALES PRODUCE TONALITY

Music based on a certain diatonic key is said to have the tonality of that key. This means that its tonal center is the tonic. The tonic of the scale seems more important, more final, than other notes. A melody based upon the key of C major, for example, seems to come to a resting place on C and often begins and ends on C. Likewise, the accompaniment may end with the chord C-E-G-C, which has the tonic as its root, thus giving the feeling of finality.

KEY SIGNATURES

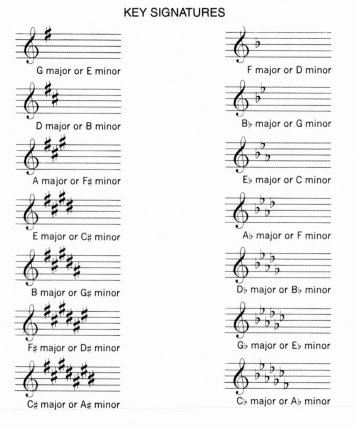

G major or E minor

D major or B minor

A major or F♯ minor

E major or C♯ minor

B major or G♯ minor

F♯ major or D♯ minor

C♯ major or A♯ minor

F major or D minor

B♭ major or G minor

E♭ major or C minor

A♭ major or F minor

D♭ major or B♭ minor

G♭ major or E♭ minor

C♭ major or A♭ minor

Having a central point of reference—the tonic—
makes it possible for the composer to create variety
and tension in his music by moving to notes not closely
related to the tonic. The notes of the diatonic scale
most closely related to the tonic—and therefore "rest"
tones—are the 3rd and 5th; the "active" tones, which
create movement, are the 2nd, 4th, 6th, and 7th.

For further variety, composers occasionally use
notes and chords from keys or scales other than the
predominant one; this is called chromaticism. For a time
they might also completely change the tonality, or key,
of the music; this is called modulation. Then they return
to the original key.

COMMON SCALE TYPES

**Pentatonic (five-note) scales are used more
widely than any other scale formation. In fact,
Western art music is one of the few traditions in
which pentatonic scales do not predominate. Their
frequency is especially notable in the Far East and
in European folk music. The most common varieties of pentatonic scales use major seconds and
minor thirds, with no half steps (anhemitonic). A
representative type could be spelled C–D–E–G–A,
for example. The pentatonic scale is so pervasive
that melodies exhibiting tetratonic (four-note)
scales often appear to be pentatonic with one**

(CONTINUED ON THE NEXT PAGE)

(*CONTINUED FROM THE PREVIOUS PAGE*)

pitch omitted. Hexatonic (six-note) scales appear rather rarely in folk music and nonliterate cultures. Examples that are known often seem to be fragments of the seven-note Western diatonic scale.

Heptatonic scales are especially prominent in the world's art-music traditions. The tone systems of India, Iran, and the West are entirely heptatonic, and seven-note scales are also present in the art music of some cultures that do not use such scales exclusively (e.g., the *ritsu* scale in Japan and the *pelog* scale in Java).

With some exceptions in both the distant and the recent past, Western art music has been based largely on one heptatonic scale, known as the diatonic scale. The origins of this scale can be traced to ancient Greece, and it has been formulated to some extent according to acoustical principles. Since the octave in Western music is normally divided into 12 equal half steps, the characteristic intervals of the diatonic scale can be constructed upon any one of the 12 pitches. Such transpositions of the scale are known as *keys*.

Before the 17th century, as many as 12 different mode permutations of the diatonic scale were in common use, but only two modes—now called *major* and *minor*—have been in general use during most of the past 300 years. The diatonic scale itself consists of five whole steps (W) and two half steps (H), with the half steps dividing the whole steps into groups of two or three. The major scale uses the sequence W–W–H–W–W–W–H, as shown in the first of the following examples, while the intervals in the minor scale are **W–H–W–W–H–W–W**, as in the second.

In actual music the minor scale is usually altered in one of two ways to create greater emphasis on particular pitches. In the harmonic minor scale (the third example shown) the seventh note is raised one half step, and in the melodic minor scale (the fourth example) both the sixth and seventh notes are raised by one half step in ascending patterns while they are

(CONTINUED ON THE NEXT PAGE)

(CONTINUED FROM THE PREVIOUS PAGE)

left unaltered in descending patterns (the fifth example).

In the 19th and 20th centuries, composers made increasing use of pitches lying outside the diatonic scale, and that tendency stimulated a variety of novel scale systems, developed as alternatives to the diatonic scale. Principles for composition within the chromatic scale (consisting of all of the 12 half steps within the octave) were first articulated by the Austrian-born composer Arnold Schoenberg early in the 20th century. Other scales have also been employed on an experimental basis. The whole-tone scale (comprising six whole steps) was used prominently by the French composer Claude Debussy and others, especially in France and England. Microtonal scales requiring intervals smaller than the conventional half step have also appeared sporadically in the 20th century. Among microtonal structures the most important, perhaps, have been scales calling for quarter tones (equal to half the distance of a half step).

OTHER SCALES

Different effects are created when music is based on other kinds of scales. The whole-tone scale has no half steps: each note in this 6-note scale is a whole step from the next. With no semitones, there is less pull to the tonic and related notes, and the music has an indefinite quality. The chromatic scale is made up of the

12 black and white keys within an octave on the piano. It can be played by starting at C and playing half steps up to the next C. Since all the tones are a half step apart, there is little feeling of a tonal center.

The 12-tone scale departs even further from tonality. For a composition based upon this atonal system, the composer arranges the 12 chromatic scale tones in a selected order, repeating no tone until all 12 have been used. This tone-row serves as the composer's scale for the piece. A less drastic modification of the older tonal system is polytonality. Here the music carries two keys at once—one group of instruments playing in one tonality while another plays in another key.

The word "scale" is sometimes used to describe musical passages consisting of a succession of consecutive scale degrees in ascending or descending patterns. It is also used to describe scalelike exercises that are practiced for the development of technical proficiency on a musical instrument. "Scale" can refer in rare instances to the ordering of some musical element other than pitch. An example is the term *Klangfarbenmelodie* used in some recent music to denote a carefully arranged succession of different tone colours.

CHAPTER TWO

MUSICAL COMPOSITION

M ost of the music composed today is built on music from the past. The reason is shear mathematics. The number of possible combinations of melody notes and chords is finite. Certain phrases of new compositions inevitably are identical to phrases contained in old compositions—and composers often are honestly unaware of the duplicity. In some new compositions, lengthy segments can be found in music archives.

Modern composers sometimes knowingly borrow passages and themes from older works that are in the public domain. Many contemporary pop songs simply have new words put to folk tunes of yesteryear. Modern classical composers, too, have borrowed from traditional music. Composers and songwriters sometimes reuse substantial portions of their own prior creations.

Musical composition is the act of conceiving a piece of music, the art of creating music, or the finished product. These meanings are interdependent and presume a tradition in which musical works exist as repeatable entities. In this sense, composition is necessarily distinct from improvisation. (Improvisation is also called extemporization, the extemporaneous composition or free performance of a musical passage, usually in a manner conforming to certain stylistic norms but unfettered by the prescriptive features of a specific musical text.)

SOCIETAL PERSPECTIVES OF MUSICAL COMPOSITION

Whether referring to the process or to the completed work, composition implies the creation of a unique musical event that may or may not be based on original musical materials. At certain cultural levels and in many non-Western societies, unique performance characteristics tend to assume greater significance than composition itself. In oral traditions, related variants of common origin often take the place of unalterable musical entities, so that tune families rather than single autonomous tunes form the collective repertoire. Where certain patterns of musical structure have gained broad recognition (as the ragas, or melody types, of India), musicians will as a rule rework such patterns extemporaneously though in accordance with prevailing conventions.

European music was communicated orally well into the Middle Ages and received important stimuli from a variety of oral traditions even after musical notation had developed to a high degree of precision. Indeed, the lower population strata, especially in rural areas, never abandoned the relative freedom that comes from reliance on the ear alone, and the sophisticated music of the upper strata, throughout its rapid evolution, rarely severed its connection with folk music altogether. Ultimately, the process of composition, as seen by the American musicologist Alan P. Merriam, does "not seem to differ radically between literate and non-literate peoples save in the question of writing." As a conscious act of social communication it always "involves learning, is subject to public acceptance and rejection, and is therefore a part of the broad learning process which contributes, in turn, to the processes of stability and change." Whether explicitly or not, composition is thus subject to rules that represent the stylistic consensus of a specific segment of society at a given stage of cultural development. During the Middle Ages, when a person's natural instincts were held in particularly low esteem, musical compositions were often judged primarily in terms of their adherence to the rules. Hence, the supreme authority in matters musical was the *musicus* as theorist; only he was considered sufficiently conversant with musical science to vouchsafe its continued existence as the sonorous embodiment of universal truths. And it was because the metaphysical properties of numbers were allegedly embedded in the rules of composition that music, on a par with arithmetic, geometry, and astronomy, attained and retained an honorable place as a constituent member of the quadrivium, the more exalted of the two divisions of the seven liberal arts. Characteristically, music was not classified with grammar, rhetoric, and logic, the "rhetorical arts" gathered in the trivium. About 1300, musical composition as a mere craft was ranked by Johannes de Grocheo, a shrewd observer of the Parisian musical scene, with shoemaking and tanning.

MUSICAL ELEMENTS

At its most fundamental level the act of composition involves the ordering of pitched sounds in musical time and space. Pitch relationships are referred to as intervals; their specific occurrence in musical time is determined by rhythm, a concept that embraces all durational aspects of music. Rhythm in turn may or may not be regulated by metre. In metrically organized rhythm, recurring patterns of accented and unaccented "beats" furnish a durational substructure that necessarily affects all the other elements of composition, including the nature of melody, harmony, and texture. Metrical rhythm is nearly always present in dance music because its patterning is largely analogous to that of bodily motions and step figurations. But logogenic, or word-determined, music also often employs metrical patterns, corresponding as a rule to those of the poetic text. The first large corpus of logogenic compositions transmitted through the ages is that of medieval plainchant, consisting of monophonic settings (limited to a single melodic line) of liturgical texts for the entire year, based on a system of eight church modes, diatonic scales abstracted from the melodic motives utilized by medieval singers. Modality—whether referring to a melodic or a rhythmic framework—furnishes compositional frames of reference in a wide variety of essentially monophonic musical styles, especially in Asia. Asian influences upon early European music cannot be ruled out, whether by way of ancient Judaea, Greece, Byzantium, or the medieval Arab invasions. Unlike their Asian counterparts, Europeans at first limited modality to melody, through pitch arrangements. The rhythmic properties of plainchant have largely remained a matter of conjecture, for no systematic discussion of plainchant rhythm survives, and the notation used was noncommittal with respect to rhythm. By the same token, plainchant no doubt owed much of its

This miniature is attributed to Lorenzo Monaco (c. 1372–c. 1424) and is from a choir book of plainchant for the Choir of Saint Romuald, Italy.

amazing vitality to the absence of an all-encompassing notation, which made possible the flexibility of performance and regional variation inherent in a partly written, partly oral tradition.

Music like medieval plainchant, in which the lengths of individual tones tend to be rather uniform, is often referred to as nonrhythmic or rhythmless. Such careless terminology denies the very essence of music as a temporal art, which implies by definition the omnipresence of rhythm as "order in musical time." Actually, the relative presence or lack of rhythmic differentiation in the duration of tones can act as a decisive stylistic determinant. Thus the rhythmic equanimity of the monophonic plainchant, at least in the interpretation set forth by the 19th-century Benedictine monks of Solesmes, France, and recognized as authoritative by the Roman Catholic Church, effectively symbolizes an atmosphere of faith and inner peace. By contrast, the strictly metrical organization of rhythm in most 18th-century music reflects the thinking of an age of reason, favouring mathematically definable, hence "natural," structures in its music.

The smallest melodic-rhythmic unit (minimally two separately perceived sounds) is the motive. Pitched sounds are, however, not of the essence: drum motives are so effective rhythmically precisely because they lack pitch definition. By and large, rhythmic motives are used to endow pitch relationships with identifiable durational characteristics. And consequently rhythmic identity often serves to establish motive connections between different intervals. A famous case in point is the opening short–short–short–long motif of Beethoven's *Symphony No. 5 in C Minor*, Opus 67, which serves as an effective element of structural cohesion in this large-scale work.

Types of melody owe their aesthetic associations in many instances to their motivic peculiarities. In Western music motivic contrast has been identified with emotional conflict since at least the mid-16th century, when composers of madrigals (Italian polyphonic secular songs) began to set dramatic texts. The opening of Mozart's *Symphony No. 35 in D Major*, K 385 (the *Haffner Symphony*), offers an excellent example. Analogous in its motivic structure to a section of the first act of Mozart's opera *Don Giovanni*, the opening of the symphony engenders emotional contrasts similar to those inherent in the opera's dramatic action when Donna Anna, under the double impact of attempted rape and her father's violent death at the Don's hands, impulsively rejects Don Ottavio's sympathy until, realizing that she has no one else to rely on for help, she reverses herself and induces him to swear revenge. Conversely, melodic lyricism correlates with a high degree of motive affinity.

THE ELEMENTS OF RHYTHM

The placement of sounds in time is known as rhythm. In its most general sense rhythm (Greek *rhythmos*, derived from *rhein*, "to flow") is an ordered alternation of contrasting elements. The notion of rhythm also occurs in other arts (e.g., poetry, painting, sculpture, and architecture) as well as in nature (e.g., biological rhythms).

Attempts to define rhythm in music have produced much disagreement, partly because rhythm has often been identified with one or more of its constituent, but not wholly separate, elements, such as accent, metre, and tempo. As in the closely related subjects of verse and metre, opinions differ widely, at least among poets and linguists, on the nature and movement of rhythm. Theories requiring "periodicity" as the *sine qua non* of rhythm are opposed by theories that include in it even nonrecurrent configurations of movement, as in prose or plainchant.

Unlike a painting or a piece of sculpture, which are compositions in space, a musical work is a composition dependent upon time. Rhythm is music's pattern in time. Whatever other elements a given piece of music may have (e.g., patterns in pitch or timbre), rhythm is the one indispensable element of all music. Rhythm can exist without melody, as in the drumbeats of primitive music, but melody cannot exist without rhythm. In music that has both harmony and melody, the rhythmic structure cannot be separated from them. Plato's observation that rhythm is "an order of movement" provides a convenient analytical starting point.

The unit division of musical time is called a beat. Just as one is aware of the body's steady

(CONTINUED ON THE NEXT PAGE)

(CONTINUED FROM THE PREVIOUS PAGE)

pulse, or heartbeat, so in composing, performing, or listening to music one is aware of a periodic succession of beats.

The pace of the fundamental beat is called *tempo* (Italian "time"). The expressions *slow tempo* and *quick tempo* suggest the existence of a tempo that is neither slow nor fast. This "moderate" tempo is often assumed to be that of a natural walking pace (76 to 80 paces per minute) or of a heartbeat (72 per minute). The tempo of a piece of music indicated by a composer is, however, neither absolute nor final. In performance it is likely to vary according to the performer's interpretative ideas or to such considerations as the size and reverberation of the hall, the size of the ensemble, and, to a lesser extent, the sonority of the instruments. A change within such limits does not affect the rhythmic structure of a work.

The tempo of a work is never inflexibly mathematical. It is impossible to adhere in a musical manner to the metronomic beat for any length of time. In a loosely knit passage a tautening of tempo may be required; in a crowded passage a slackening may be needed. Such modifications of tempo, known as *tempo rubato*–i.e., "robbed time"–are part of the music's character. Rubato needs the framework of an inflexible beat from which it can depart and to which it must return.

DEVELOPMENT OF COMPOSITION IN THE MIDDLE AGES

The European written tradition, largely because it evolved under church auspices, de-emphasized rhythmic distinctiveness long after multipart music had superseded the monophonic plainchant. But multipart music might never have gone beyond the most primitive stages of counterpoint had it not been for the application of organized rhythm to musical structure in the late Middle Ages. This era witnessed the emergence of basic polyphonic concepts identified with European art music ever since. The precise measurement of musical time was simply an indispensable prerequisite for compositions in which separate, yet simultaneously sounded, melodic entities were combined in accordance with the medieval theorists' rules of consonance (specifying the proper intervals to be used between voice parts, especially at points of musical repose). Toward the end of the 1st millennium of the Christian Era, church singers had grown accustomed to enhancing their chants through organum. "Parallel" organum was followed, in turn, by "free" organum, which allowed the synchronized voice parts to utilize contrary melodic motion.

The decisive relationship between text and melody in early European music led to stylistic distinctions that have survived the ages. Thus, "syllabic" denotes a setting where one syllable corresponds to one note; "melismatic" refers to a phrase or composition employing several distinct pitches for the vocalization of a single syllable. Late medieval composers made clever use of these distinctions, including an intermediate "neumatic" style (Greek *pneuma*, "breath") to create ever more extensive polyphonic pieces. By the 12th century musicians at Notre-Dame in Paris, led by Léonin, the first polyphonic composer known by name, cultivated a type of melismatic organum that featured a highly florid upper part above a slow moving cantus firmus taken from a suitable plainchant melody. The melismatic sections alternated with strictly measured, or "discant," sections. This very effective procedure possibly was inspired by Middle Eastern practices with which the crusaders must have been well acquainted. In Eastern music, the rhythmically measured portions following the virtuoso singer's florid "outpouring of the soul" are nearly always played or at least supported by instruments. In the 13th century the *clausula*, a short, textless composition in descant style, tended to be dancelike in its systematic sectionalization, strongly suggesting instrumental derivation if not necessarily actual performance. The motet, a major genre of the medieval and Renaissance eras, was in its 13th-century form essentially a texted clausula, frequently employing two or three different texts in as many languages. This fact merely reinforces the suspicion that little distinction was made between vocal and instrumental composition in an era that so blithely based dancelike settings of erotic, in a few instances outright obscene, texts on a chant-derived cantus firmus. The point is not without its broader ramifications. For, brought up largely on 19th-century notions about the "purity" of church music, one easily overlooks the fact that even Bach and Mozart had few compunctions about the use of secular—in their cases mostly operatic—styles and specific tunes in church music. Over the centuries, the church has been the most important employer of composers and has offered far greater outlets for newly created music than any other social institution or category. Thus, composers of sacred music have had to satisfy the aesthetic needs and expectations of its highly differentiated "public." The church in turn repeatedly permitted the adaptation of promising secular types of composition, even though instrumental music, because of its more lascivious associations, remained suspect well into the 17th century.

In accordance with medieval tendencies generally, Gothic polyphonic music was conceived in loosely connected separate layers. Thus, two-part motets could be converted into three-part motets, and Léonin's successor Pérotin expanded the organum to three and four parts. Inevitably, as their compositions gained in length and depth, musicians began to search for new integrative procedures. A system of six rhythmic modes (short, repeated rhythmic patterns) evolved rapidly. Pérotin used a single rhythmic mode for the multiple upper parts of his organums so that, separated from their cantus firmus, they resembled the conductus, a syllabic setting of a sacred text for two or three voices sharing the same basic rhythm. Finally, as organum faded into history, conductus-type motets were composed outright. Most prominent among the devices used to achieve structural integration in the 13th century were colour, or melodic repetition without regard to rhythmic organization; talea, or rhythmic repetition without regard to pitch organization; and ostinato, or repetition of a relatively brief melodic-rhythmic pattern. Exchanges of melodic phrases between two or more parts in turn led to canon, a form in which all voice parts are derived from one tune—either by strict imitation of the basic melody or by manipulations stipulated in often quite sophisticated verbal instructions (canon = law). For instance, the canon *Ma fin est mon commencement* (*My End Is My Beginning*), by Guillaume de Machaut, the leading French composer of the 14th century, demands the simultaneous performance of a melody and its retrograde version (the notes are sung in reverse order). French musicians of the 14th century were particularly partial to isorhythm which refers to repetition of the rhythmic organization of all the voices in a given compositional segment. It enjoyed considerable popularity for more than 100 years.

Meanwhile, though somewhat eclipsed historically by the increasingly abstract nature of polyphony, the primacy of poetry was safeguarded in 13th-century music by the troubadours of southern France and their northern counterparts, the trouvères, as well as the German Minnesingers. These noble poet-composers created a rich tradition of purely monophonic secular song that furnished convenient points of departure for much of the secular polyphonic music in both 14th-century France and 15th-century Germany. By the beginning of the 15th century, European music had also begun to feel the impact of English music. The English emphasis on the rich sonorities of the third and sixth provided welcome relief from the aesthetic consequences of the earlier continental dedication to the "perfect" intervals of the octave, fourth, and fifth. Because the perfect intervals were also those formed by the lowest pitches of the harmonic overtone series, their "naturalness" had long been an unassailable theoretical axiom.

Late 14th-century French secular music virtually lost itself in rhythmic complexities without any substantive changes in the basic compositional approach, which continued to favour relatively brief three-part settings of lyrical poetry. But in the ensuing 15th century the simpler melodic and rhythmic ideas associated with the rich harmonies of the English style were eagerly embraced; often melodies were outright triadic in contour; i.e., they outlined the intervals of the triad, an increasingly important chord composed of two linked thirds (e.g., C-E-G). But the truly amazing stylistic development from the influential English composer John Dunstable to Josquin des Prez, the French-Flemish composer who stands at the apex of his era, was equally indebted to the flowing cantilenas, or lyric melodies, that characterized the top parts of Italian trecento music. If the French music of the waning Middle Ages was structured essentially from the bottom up, with relatively angular melodic and rhythmic patterns above the two-dimensional substructure of tenor and countertenor, its Italian counterparts were quite often monodically conceived; i.e., a highly singable tune was sparingly yet effectively supported by a single lower voice. Indeed, the passion for melody, if need be to the detriment of other musical elements, has been a constant of Italian music. It sparked the *nuove musiche*, or "new music," of about 1600 and is exemplified in innumerable works of composers as diverse as Claudio Monteverdi (1567–1643) and Luigi Dallapiccola (1904–75). But it found its first major artistic expression in the city-states of northern Italy during the lifetimes of such 14th-century literary figures as Giovanni Boccaccio and Petrarch.

COMPOSITION IN THE RENAISSANCE

During the latter part of the 15th century, French rhythmic sophistication, Italian cantilena, and English harmony finally found common ground in the style of Renaissance polyphony that, under the aegis of Flemish musicians, dominated Europe for nearly two centuries. Often referred to as modal because it retained the medieval system of melodic modes, Flemish polyphony was characterized by a highly developed sense of structure and textural integration. Although the older cantus firmus technique was never totally abandoned, Renaissance polyphony is identified above all with imitative part writing, inspired no doubt by earlier canonic procedures but devoid of their structural limitations. After a canonic or freely imitational beginning, each of the subunits of such a polyphonic piece proceeds unfettered by canonic restrictions, yet preserves the fundamental equality of the melodic lines in accordance with contrapuntal rules amply discussed by various 15th- and 16th-century theorists and ultimately codified by the Italian theorist Gioseffo Zarlino. Through the works of Giovanni da Palestrina, the model composer of the Catholic Counter-Reformation, Renaissance modal counterpoint has influenced the teaching of musical composition to the present, suggesting the near perfection with which it conveys some fundamental aspects of the historic European ideal of composition as the art of lasting musical structures.

Whereas imitative polyphony affected virtually all 16th-century music, modal counterpoint was paramount in sacred pieces, specifically the motet and mass, probably because of its close kinship with the traditional modality of liturgical plainchant. In contrast, the beginnings of functional harmony (chordal relationships governed by primary and secondary tonal centres) manifested themselves first in the polyphonic French chanson; its Italian counterpart, the madrigal; and related secular types. Under the influence of less sophisticated music, such as that of the Italian frottola, a popular vocal genre, these secular polyphonic genres favoured rather simple bass lines highlighting a limited number of related harmonies. Thus, undisturbed by the theoretical writings from the pens of church-employed musicians, secular musical practice in the later Renaissance laid the foundations for the harmonic notions that were to dominate three centuries of Western art music. The increasing emotionalism of texts taken from the leading Italian poet of the 16th century, Torquato Tasso, and his immediate successors acted as a further stimulant, as Italian composers, searching for appropriate musical symbols, discovered the expressive possibilities of chordal progressions.

THE BAROQUE PERIOD

Inevitably, the strong desire for heightened expression through harmony led at first to new, mostly chromatic, chord progressions. Eventually it precipitated the total abandonment of traditional polyphony about 1600 in the monodic experiments of the Florentine Camerata, a group of aristocratic connoisseurs seeking to emulate the Greek drama of antiquity. The accompaniment for these passionate and heroic solo recitations is based on a simple basso continuo. Only the bass part was written down; it was played by low, sustaining instruments bowed or blown, while plucked or keyboard instruments supplied the chords suggested by the bass and melody lines. The small figures used to indicate the proper harmonies gave the system the alternative name figured bass. Monody had its historical antecedents in mid-16th-century solo lute songs and in the plentiful arrangements of polyphonic vocal compositions for single voices accompanied by plucked instruments and for solo keyboard instruments. But it was the attempt to resurrect the spirit of antique drama in the late Renaissance that created the textural revolution that has been equated with the beginnings of modern music: the monodic style with its polarity of bass and melody lines and emphasis on chords superseded the equal-voiced polyphonic texture of Renaissance music. Monteverdi, the undisputed master of the monodic style, recognized the possibility of two basic approaches to composition: the first, or polyphonic, "practice" and the second, or monodic, "practice." Thus, with penetrating analytical insight he formulated the basic stylistic dialectic that has since governed the course of Western music. The emergence of an essentially nonpolyphonic style went hand-in-hand with the rise of a variety of specifically instrumental idioms. Not only did accompanied vocal music offer instrumentalists various opportunities for improvisation; the basically chordal style also facilitated the emergence of virtuosity in the modern sense of the term, especially among keyboard artists. But as the singer and composer Giulio Caccini demonstrated in the preface to his influential collection *Le nuove musiche* (*The New Music*; 1602), singers, too, put their newly found freedom to good improvisational and ornamentational use. In short, after two centuries dominated by the highly structured, rationalistic polyphony of the Renaissance, the performing musician reiterated his creative rights. Inevitably, under such forceful pressures, the teaching of composition, previously tied to the laws of modal counterpoint, quickly shifted to the harmonic challenges of the figured bass.

Because the bass-oriented music of the 17th century relied primarily on chord progressions as fixed by the bass notes, it was structurally quite open-ended; i.e., the new technique suited any number of formal patterns. Even so, the incipient rationalism that was to reach its peak in the 18th century soon led to the consolidation of broadly accepted structural types. Indeed, the very concept of musical "form," as generally understood from the late 17th century on, was intimately tied to the growing importance of instrumental music, which, in the absence of a text, had nothing to rely upon save its own organically developed laws. At least for a while, vocal music, which had been so largely responsible for the monodic revolution, continued to adhere to the Monteverdian principle that the words must act as "the mistress of harmony." Both melody and harmony, therefore, reflected often minute affective textual differentiations. And as late as the early 18th century similar musico-rhetorical considerations led to *Affektenlehre*, the theory of musical affects (emotions, feelings), developed primarily in Germany. Following this theory, German musicians dealt with composition systematically in terms of a specific but broadly adopted expressive vocabulary of melodic, rhythmic, and harmonic figures. Meanwhile, the Italians laid the foundations for such lasting categories of instrumental music as the symphony, the sonata, and the concerto. In each instance the structural outline was harmonically determined through juxtapositions of principal key areas acting as focal centres of tonality. As for tempo, the earliest 17th-century solo sonatas had relied on drastic short-range changes in accordance with a general predilection for "instant sensations." Subsequently, as musical composition fell in line with the prevailing rationalistic trend, tempo served above all as a means of differentiation between the various movements, or self-contained sections, that constituted the large-scale works of the Italian string school and of French and German instrumental composers as well. Texture, too, was used to provide contrast, particularly within a given movement, as in the concerto grosso with its alternation between small and large groups of players (concertino and tutti).

Interrelated with the spectacular rise and amazing vitality of instrumental music was its unprecedented variety. By the early 18th century, composers drew freely upon everything from contrapuntal forms like the fugue (an adaptation of the imitative techniques of the Renaissance motet within the context of functional harmony) to stylized popular dances, such as those that make up the suites and partitas of J.S. Bach. The figured bass era took full advantage of the possibilities of variety and contrast through judicious manipulations of all elements of composition. Whereas accompanied solo music pitted bass against treble (the latter often split up into two parts, as in the trio sonata), composers generally liked to juxtapose figured bass and polyphonic textures. Melodically, the far-flung phrases of Italian bel canto, the florid singing style characteristic of opera seria (17th- and 18th-century tragic opera), had little in common with the concise, symmetrically balanced phrases found in music of popular inspiration, whether in opera buffa (Italian comic opera) or the many types of dances. As for the latter, their impact on sophisticated 18th-century music is evident not only in many dance-inspired arias and concerto movements but also in certain polyphonic compositions. Both the chaconne and passacaglia, related polyphonic types, were based on dancelike ostinato patterns, often with specific harmonic implications. Perhaps the most famous example is Bach's "Chaconne" for solo violin, which concludes the *Partita in D Minor*.

Even though the Baroque preoccupation with style worked somewhat to the detriment of structural definition, certain closed forms did gradually emerge. The da capo aria distinguished clearly between an initial section (A), a contrasting section (B), and the repeat (da capo) of the initial section, as a rule with improvised vocal embellishment. In instrumental music, the French opera overture began with a slow, stately introduction followed by a fast, often fugal movement, whereas its Italian counterpart had a tripartite fast-slow-fast scheme. Dance-based suite movements were binary in outline: the first of the two sections, each separately repeated, moved to the dominant key (a fifth above the tonic or principal key) or to the relative key (i.e., a minor third above the tonic in the case of a minor key); the second section, after some modulatory activity (i.e., passing through several key areas), returned to the central key. Even more decisive in its far-reaching historical consequences was the structural organization of a number of the keyboard "sonatas" of the composer Domenico Scarlatti. These works consisted of single, essentially binary movements, the first section of which differentiated not only between two key areas but two contrasting thematic ideas as well.

THE CLASSICAL PERIOD

The Classical era in music is compositionally defined by the balanced eclecticism of the late 18th- and early 19th-century Viennese "school" of Haydn, Mozart, Beethoven, and Schubert, who completely absorbed and individually fused or transformed the vast array of 18th-century textures and formal types. Expansion of the tripartite Italian overture had produced the basic three-movement scheme of the symphony even before the 18th century reached midpoint. Shortly thereafter, the minuet, borrowed from the dance suite, was inserted with increasing frequency as a fourth movement between the slow movement and the fast finale. The French opera overture in turn lent its slow introduction where needed for structural variety. Texturally, homophony (chordal texture) and polyphony soon assumed rather specific roles, with polyphonic writing usually reserved for the central or development section of the classical first-movement form. The organic fusion of a number of stylistic traits previously associated with strong and immediate contrast is exemplified by the obbligato accompaniment, the texture most typical of

Viennese classicism. Here the relative equality of all the melodic parts in a given composition is ensured without denying the melodic supremacy of the treble and the harmonically decisive role of the bass. The evolution of this characteristic texture can be traced in the string quartets of Haydn. At first, following earlier 18th-century custom, Haydn wrote strictly treble-dominated compositions with a simplified bass (as compared with the more varied basso continuo); then, with the six *Sun Quartets*, Opus 20, dating from the early 1770s, he defied precedent and concluded each work with a fugue in the "learned style" of Handel. Finally, in his *Russian Quartets*, Opus 33, written, in his own words, "in a new manner," Haydn achieved the fusion of elements of both the learned and the treble-dominated styles. The result was a harmonically oriented, yet polyphonically animated, texture that was to affect both instrumental and vocal ensemble music for generations. It was also at this point, when compositional procedures reached a degree of stability and universality unmatched since Renaissance polyphony, that composition began to be taken seriously as a separate musicianly discipline. Johann Joseph Fux's famous *Gradus ad Parnassum* (*Steps to Parnassus*), published first in Latin in 1725 and subsequently in every important modern language, was still basically a didactic treatise on counterpoint abstracted from 16th-century practice. As such it served its purpose throughout the 18th century, while harmony continued to be taught as the art of accompaniment—i.e., the improvised realization of a figured bass. But eventually the general fascination with comprehensive knowledge, sparked by the French *Encyclopédie*, inspired at first sporadic, then ever more numerous, volumes dealing progressively with all aspects of composition. During the ensuing 19th century the rapid institutionalization of musical education in the image of the National Conservatory of Music in Paris, created while the French Revolution was still raging, added further to the academic systematization of all musical studies along lines that have essentially remained in force. Thus the teaching of musical composition reflects to this day the biases of the 19th century, specifically its concern with functional harmony as the principal generative force

Franz Joseph Haydn (1732–1809) is depicted conducting and playing with a string quartet in Vienna, Austria.

in music—a doctrine first proclaimed in the 1720s in the name of nature (as being consistent with the harmonic overtone series) by the composer and theorist Jean-Philippe Rameau.

THE ROMANTIC PERIOD

With the onset of the Romantic era in the wake of the French Revolution, composers began to view their own role in society as well as the social function of their work, and hence also its aesthetic prerequisites, in a radically different light. With respect to social function, Beethoven was actually the first musician of stature to achieve emancipation in the sense that his work reflected, with relatively few exceptions, purely personal artistic concerns. He simply took it for granted that patrons would supply funds sufficient for him to pursue his creative career unfettered by financial worries. This attitude represents a total reversal of the basic assumptions of the preceding century, when composers were hired by and large to satisfy the musical needs of specific individuals or institutions.

The view of the composer as artist also changed. If during the Middle Ages the craft of musical composition had been evaluated largely in terms of its strict adherence to established rules, instinctiveness and spontaneity had remained suspect well into the Italian Renaissance. For a 15th-century composer-theorist like Johannes Tinctoris, the value of a musical composition depended on learned judgment as well as spontaneous reaction. Thus his admiration for certain composers of his time stemmed both from the happiness and from the enlightenment that he found in examining their music. But the Swiss theorist Henricus Glareanus, writing 70 years later, explicitly preferred natural talent to the most exquisite craftsmanship. The Renaissance was the first epoch in European intellectual history to recognize that the greatness of a composer rests upon his inherent talent and unique personal style, and that genius supersedes both experience and the observance of theoretical precepts. Likewise, it was the first era in which the process of composition was viewed as linked to powerful internal impulses. The rising tide of academicism notwithstanding, this basic attitude on the whole dominated the European scene more or less consistently from then on. According to E.T.A. Hoffmann, the early 19th-century poet, critic, and composer, "effective composition is nothing but the art of capturing with a higher strength, and fixing in the hieroglyphs of tones, what was received in the mind's unconscious ecstasis." And Romantic composers from Robert Schumann and Frédéric Chopin to Hugo Wolf and Gustav Mahler did in fact produce much of their very best creative work in precisely such a state of exaltation, in a few tragic instances (e.g., Schumann and Wolf) to the ultimate detriment of their sanity.

The aesthetic effects of this drastic change in conception of the composer's task and potential were immediate and far reaching. For one, every large-scale composition assumed artistic significance of a type previously accorded only a whole series of works, sometimes a composer's entire output. And, concomitantly, many leading composers of the 19th century wrote in considerably smaller quantities than their predecessors. But in exchange they revelled in idiomatic and structural peculiarities even in works that nominally fell into the same formal category. Thus, although "characteristic" symphonies alluding to nonmusical ideas occurred occasionally in the late 18th century, virtually every symphonic composition postdating Beethoven's *Symphony No. 3 in E Flat Major*, Opus 55 (*Eroica*; completed 1804), could be so designated. "Characteristic" works like Beethoven's *Symphony No. 6 in F Major*, Opus 68 (*Pastoral*; 1808), or his overture to J.W. Goethe's *Egmont* (1810) are but one step removed from the kind of characteristic scenes that make up the *Symphonie fantastique* (1830) of the French composer Hector Berlioz or, for that matter, Felix Mendelssohn's *Hebrides* (also known as *Fingal's Cave* [1830–32]), an overture unrelated to any particular drama, spoken or sung. Franz Liszt, in the freewheeling forms of his symphonic poems, simply pursued the individualistic line to its ultimate consequences, severing whatever tenuous ties to traditional structures the works of his immediate predecessors had still maintained. The Romantic composer viewed himself basically as a poet who manipulated musical sounds instead of words. But if the composers catered to poetry, writing lieder (German songs) and attempting to retell stories in instrumental works, the poets looked with awe and envy upon the composers' use of a language so utterly dissociated from material existence. "All art aspires to the condition of music," said Wordsworth. It is thus hardly surprising that opera, whose extramusical connotations had in the past been responsible for some of the most daring stylistic innovations, rapidly incurred the disfavour of progressive composers. Although some, like Berlioz, Mendelssohn, and Schumann, tried their hands at an occasional opera, others, including Chopin, Liszt, and Brahms, felt no inclination whatever to compose for the stage. Instead, each developed personal idioms capable of a depth of expression that words could not match. Mendelssohn spoke indeed for many when he remarked that, as far as he was concerned, music was more precise in meaning than words.

As in the late Renaissance, harmony once again furnished the primary expressive means. In defining musical structure, too, harmonic and modulatory procedures predominated at the expense of the contrapuntal interplay of motives. Numerous Romantic composers excelled in concise forms of strong melodic-harmonic import, variously entitled *Impromptu, Nocturne, Song Without Words, Ballade, Capriccio, Prelude, Étude*, etc. The form of these works was nearly always tripartite, with a literal or modified repeat of the first part following a melodically and harmonically contrasting middle section. Works of larger scope often consisted of a series of relatively autonomous subunits tied together either by the same tune presented in different guises (as in variation sets) or by fairly literal recurrences of an initial musical idea (the rondo principle). Compositions of the Classical sonata-allegro type, to which motivic-contrapuntal development was essential, inevitably suffered from the Romantic love for pure, harmonically defined melody. Thus Pyotr Ilyich Tchaikovsky frankly admitted in 1878 that, although he could not complain of poverty of imagination or lack of inventive power, his lack of structural skill had frequently caused his "seams" to show: "there was no organic union between my individual episodes." Composers such as Tchaikovsky were indeed particularly successful with chainlike formations like the serenade or the ballet suite, which comprised a well-calculated number of carefully wrought smaller entities.

In the context of functional harmony, the Classical motivic-contrapuntal approach had no doubt been exploited in the last sonatas and string quartets of Beethoven to the very limits of its potential to define musical structure. The heroic image of Beethoven as one who had overcome every possible personal and artistic difficulty to achieve the highest aims of the art assumed well-nigh traumatic proportions among 19th-century musicians. Not only did composers ill-equipped both by training and artistic temperament try to emulate him, but theorists from Adolf Bernhard Marx to Vincent d'Indy based treatises on his works. Thus, unwittingly the Classical Beethovenian inheritance turned into something of an aesthetic liability for Romantic composers swayed by the image of Beethoven and unable or unwilling to face the fact that their particular talents were totally unsuited for any further capitalization of his basic compositional procedures. Confronted with the task of writing in the Beethovenian manner, a great master like Schumann, who had created the near-perfect, totally Romantic suite *Carnaval*, Opus 9 (1835), was clearly out of his element: the development of his *Symphony No. 1 in B Flat Major*, Opus 38 (also called the *Spring Symphony*) (1841), offers a prime example of the "rhythmic paralysis" that affected so many large-scale 19th-century works. That this symphony managed nevertheless to maintain itself in the concert repertoire, on the other hand, demonstrates the extent to which the best among the German composers compensated for obvious weaknesses in handling motivic development by sustaining above all constant harmonic interest. For their part, the French, always colouristically inclined, turned instrumentation into a principal compositional resource, so that in an unadorned piano transcription Berlioz's *Symphonie fantastique* retains little more than its basic contours. That by the end of the century virtuoso instrumentation had become universal practice is attested by any work of Richard Strauss or Gustav Mahler.

Characteristically, the most unique compositional achievement of the 19th century, that of Richard Wagner, was also the most eclectic. Wagner represents the apotheosis of Romanticism in music precisely because he fused into musico-poetic structures of unprecedented proportions virtually every musical resource that went before him. Seen in this light it may be more than mere coincidence that *Tristan und Isolde* (1865), perhaps Wagner's most perfect music drama, begins with the same four notes that make up the motivic substance of four of Beethoven's string quartets (Opuses 130–133). Unlike most instrumental composers after Beethoven, the dramatist Wagner fully assimilated the motivic-contrapuntal process, even though his texture is principally determined by strong harmonic tensions and by a masterful use of instrumental colour in the vein of Berlioz and French grand opera. Just as he integrated diverse compositional techniques, Wagner also achieved a balance of musical and poetic elements so perfect that critics, both favourable and unfavourable, have never ceased to be puzzled by its aesthetic implications. How consciously Wagner proceeded is attested not only by his numerous theoretical writings but also by compositional sketches pointing in some instances to several stages of mutual adjustments involving music and text.

INSTRUMENTATION

Instrumentation is also called orchestration. It is an arrangement or composition for instruments. Most authorities make little distinction between the words *instrumentation* and *orchestration*. Both deal with musical instruments and their capabilities of producing various timbres or colours. Orchestration is somewhat the narrower term, since it is frequently used to describe the art of instrumentation as related to the symphony orchestra. Instrumentation, therefore, is the art of combining instruments in any sort of musical composition, including such diverse elements as the numerous combinations used in chamber groups, jazz bands, rock ensembles, ensembles employing chorus, symphonic bands, and, of course, the symphony orchestra.

In Western music there are many standard or traditional groups. Although there is great variability, depending on the composer and the era, a modern symphony orchestra often comprises the following instruments:

1. Woodwinds: three flutes, piccolo, three oboes, English horn, three clarinets, bass clarinet, three bassoons, contrabassoon (double bassoon).

(*CONTINUED ON THE NEXT PAGE*)

(*CONTINUED FROM THE PREVIOUS PAGE*)

2. Brass: four trumpets, four or five horns, three trombones, tuba.
3. Strings: two harps, first and second violins, violas, violoncellos, double basses.
4. Percussion: four timpani (played by one player), several other instruments (shared by a group of players).

The orchestra has arrived at this complement through centuries of evolution; the present size is needed to perform music from the Baroque, Classical, and Romantic periods, as well as the varied repertoires that followed.

The various sections, with the exception of percussion, divide themselves in somewhat the same manner as a choir. The woodwinds, for example, divide into flutes (sopranos), oboes (altos), clarinets (tenors), and bassoons (basses), although this distinction must be greatly qualified. Instrumental range is larger than vocal range, and the clarinets of an orchestra may play higher than the flutes in a woodwind passage.

The standard instrumental groups of Western chamber music include the string quartet (two violins, viola, and violoncello), the woodwind quintet (flute, oboe, clarinet, horn, and bassoon), the combinations employed in sonatas (one wind or stringed instrument with piano), and the brass quintet (frequently two trumpets, horn, trombone, and tuba).

In addition to these standard groups there are, however, hundreds of other possible combinations.

Other groups that deserve mention are those used in popular music. The dance band, popular in the 1930s and 1940s, consisted of five saxophones, four trumpets, four trombones, double bass, piano, guitar, and drums. The basic rock ensemble consists of two electric guitars, electric bass, electronic keyboard, drums, and frequently one or more singers. The concert band, which is particularly popular in North America, consists of mixed wind and percussion players totalling from about 40 to well beyond 100 players.

Types of instrumentation
The approach to the art of instrumentation is naturally greatly influenced by the type of group for which the composer is writing. A string quartet or a group of brass instruments, for instance, cannot be treated in the same manner as a symphony orchestra. In general, the larger and more diverse the instrumental group, the more colouristic possibilities it presents to the composer. The smaller instrumental groups often have a sound character of their own, and the composer is challenged to find new and interesting ways to deal with this limitation.

The symphony orchestra has had definite traditions in relation to orchestration. The

(CONTINUED ON THE NEXT PAGE)

(*CONTINUED FROM THE PREVIOUS PAGE*)

composer of the 18th century was likely to use the orchestral instruments at least part of the time in the following manner: the flutes doubling the same part as the first violins (frequently the melody); the oboes doubling the second violins or the first violins in octaves; the clarinets (by the end of the century) doubling the violas; and the bassoons doubling the violoncellos and double basses. Horns were often used as harmonic "filler" and in conjunction with every section of the orchestra because of their ability to blend easily with both stringed and wind instruments.

These traditional doublings were not so often used in the orchestration of the 19th and 20th centuries because of the great improvement in the making of wind instruments and their consequent ability to function in a solo capacity. Wind instruments became used more and more for colouring; the flutes, for instance, were noted for their bright tone quality and great technical agility, the clarinets for all the aforementioned qualities, and the bassoons for their special tone quality. Brass instruments had to await the development of valves, which increased greatly the musical proficiency of brass players and overcame previous typecasting of these instruments as bugles and hunting horns.

String techniques
The string quartet has long been considered one of the greatest challenges to the composer

Presidential Medal of Freedom recipient cellist Yo-Yo Ma (*seated, left*) performs in 2011 with the Marine Band String Quartet at the White House in Washington, D.C.

because the contrast to be achieved by changing from one type of instrument when writing for a full orchestra is simply not available. The composer has had to rely on varying timbres to be arrived at by different playing techniques, such as pizzicato (plucking the strings), tremolo (the quick reiteration of the same tone), sul ponticello (bowing near the bridge of the instrument), sul tasto (bowing on the fingerboard), the use of harmonics (dividing the string in such a way as to produce a high flutelike tone), col legno (striking the strings with the wood of the bow), and many special bowing techniques.

(CONTINUED ON THE NEXT PAGE)

(*CONTINUED FROM THE PREVIOUS PAGE*)

Wind techniques

Special playing techniques also can alter the timbres of wind instruments. For instance, on many, tremolos can be played on two different notes. Some wind instruments–and the flute is particularly agile in this respect–can produce harmonics. Flutter tonguing (produced by a rapid rolling movement of the tongue) is possible on most wind instruments; so are many other tonguing techniques that affect the quality of sound in orchestration.

Percussion instrumentation

Percussion instruments became a favourite source of colour in the 20th century, in both the concert and popular fields. Instruments from all over the world are now commonly available and are divided into two categories: of definite and of indefinite pitch. The former include the xylophone, marimba, vibraphone, glockenspiel, timpani, and chimes. Instruments of indefinite pitch exist by the hundreds. Some of the more common ones are the snare drum, tenor drum, tom-tom, bass drum, bongos, Latin American timbales, many types of cymbals, maracas, claves, triangles, gongs, and temple blocks.

The availability of these instruments and the great improvement in percussion playing has resulted in an enormous increase in the number of compositions for percussion instruments. The percussion ensemble, a group of from four to eight players, is a type of chamber group that began its existence only in the 20th century, particularly since the late 1940s. One of the interesting features of such an ensemble is that each player in it is capable of playing many instruments. An ensemble of four players, for instance, can easily handle 25 or 30 instruments, once again showing the rich palette available in a single composition.

Keyboard instrumentation
Since the 17th century, keyboard instruments have played an important role in orchestration. Those commonly available today are the harpsichord, celesta, organ (both pipe and electronic), and electric piano, in addition to the instrument for which most of the standard literature has been written—the piano. Keyboard instruments vary greatly in the manner in which they produce a sound: the harpsichord has quills that pluck the strings; the piano has hammers that strike the strings; the celesta has hammers that strike a metal bar; the pipe organ sends air through a pipe; the electronic organ employs electronic oscillators to produce its sound. The resulting colours are naturally very different.

The piano, with its wide range (more than seven octaves), has been used in conjunction

(CONTINUED ON THE NEXT PAGE)

(CONTINUED FROM THE PREVIOUS PAGE)

with virtually every instrument and instrumental combination. In the 18th century it gradually replaced the harpsichord as the common keyboard instrument because of the piano's ability to alter dynamics rapidly and its ability to sustain sounds. There is a vast amount of literature for the piano as the accompanying instrument in sonatas, partly because the piano can function as a "one-person orchestra." Many composers of the 20th century discovered facets of the piano that had been previously ignored. The inside of the grand piano is a harplike body that has presented many new possibilities to the composer, such as the "prepared" piano. To prepare a piano, objects such as bolts, pennies, and erasers are inserted between the strings, thus producing many different sounds. The piano strings can be plucked or played with percussion mallets and can produce harmonics in the manner of non-keyboard stringed instruments, much to the dismay of piano tuners and traditional pianists.

Electronic instrumentation

The electric piano is one of a number of instruments that have gained in popularity since the mid-20th century. These instruments either produce sound by means of electronic oscillators or are amplified acoustic instruments. The sound produced by ensembles playing this type of instrument is distinctive. The rock ensemble is the best known, but rock musicians are by no means the only instrumentalists to employ electric instruments. For the composer, amplified or electric instruments pose certain problems. Balances can be achieved or ruined simply by turning an amplifier up or down. The timbres produced by rock ensembles and other groups employing electronics are unusual for a number of reasons. The electric guitar has such devices as reverberation controls, "wa-wa" pedals, and filters that enable the performer to change timbre radically in the middle of a performance. Composers since the early 1960s, being much concerned with colouristic possibilities of instruments, have found the electronic ones most attractive.

Vocal instrumentation

The largest quantity of literature in Western music has been written for the chorus. The choir, an instrument capable of great subtleties of colour, has been a favourite of composers for centuries. The range of most individual singing voices is rather limited. Choral singers, who usually have a limited amount of training, are capable of a range of about an octave and a fifth, which is considerably smaller than the range of individual instruments. Singers are usually not capable of singing wide leaps, that is to say, notes that are far apart in range. Great skill is required

(CONTINUED ON THE NEXT PAGE)

(CONTINUED FROM THE PREVIOUS PAGE)

in the musical setting of the text in a choral work. Attention must be paid to the vocal qualities of vowel sounds as well as to the way in which the consonants are treated.

For centuries composers have been intrigued with the combination of voices and instruments, and many of the most important compositions in Western music have been written for chorus and orchestra. Almost every major composer of the past three centuries has written for choir and large instrumental ensembles.

Western instrumentation

The development of the art of using instruments for their individual properties did not really begin in Western music until about 1600. The known history of musical instruments, however, has been traced back 40,000 years, although nothing is known about the music these early instruments produced. The Greeks left mostly musical theories and only a small amount of extant music. The Romans used instruments particularly in military bands, but, again, little is known of their specific use. The music of the Middle Ages and Renaissance was primarily vocal, although instruments were frequently used in compositions to accompany or reinforce the individual vocal line. Stringed, brass, woodwind, and percussion instruments were added not so much for their colouristic potential but because of their availability. Another practice in the Middle Ages was to make literal instrumental versions of vocal compositions, which, of course, has rather little in common with the modern art of instrumentation.

The Baroque period

Orchestration in a modern sense probably began in the 16th century with Giovanni Gabrieli, organist of St. Mark's in Venice. He was the first composer to sometimes designate specific instruments for each part in a composition, as in his *Sacrae symphoniae* (1597). Claudio Monteverdi made important contributions to the art of orchestration. His opera *Orfeo* was first performed at Mantua in 1607 with an orchestra of about 40 instruments, including flutes, cornetts, trumpets, trombones, strings, and keyboard instruments. For the first time, a composer, in order to heighten certain dramatic moments, specified exactly which instruments were to be used.

The century after the first performance of *Orfeo* was characterized by a rise in the use of stringed instruments that were similar to the modern ones. Although that trend helped set the stage for the modern orchestra, it was not a period that made great strides in the

(CONTINUED ON THE NEXT PAGE)

(CONTINUED FROM THE PREVIOUS PAGE)

art of orchestration: the prevalent practice of writing out only the melody and the bass line of a composition did not lend itself easily to creative scoring. By the end of the 17th century, however, the groundwork had been laid for new developments. Instruments and instrumentalists had improved steadily. Johann Sebastian Bach created works that occasionally exploited the colouristic capabilities of instruments but in a rather limited way. In some of Bach's music the stringed instruments are played pizzicato, although this practice had already been employed by Monteverdi. Bach also wrote for muted strings. Wind instruments were treated occasionally for their special sounds, although more frequently they were simply employed on a musical line that their range happened to fit.

George Frideric Handel, whose life covered the same period as Bach's, had a keener sense of orchestral effect. He introduced the clarinet into his orchestra, although it was not to become standard until the 19th century, and in his operas Handel often used instrumental colour in a way that did not become common practice until much later. Jean-Philippe Rameau, the leading French composer of the 18th century, also contributed much to the development of orchestration. Rameau, like Handel, was principally famous as an opera composer, and the overtures and dances of his operas represent the most advanced uses of instruments during that period. Rameau was probably the first composer to treat each instrument of the orchestra as a separate entity, and he introduced interesting and unexpected passages for flutes, oboes, and bassoons.

By the middle of the 18th century the symphony orchestra was beginning to resemble the modern instrumental group, yet it was still considerably smaller. The orchestra at the court of Mannheim, Germany, consisted of 20 violins, four violas, four cellos, two double basses, two flutes, two oboes, two bassoons, four horns, one trumpet, and kettledrums. Baroque composers frequently could not count on a fixed orchestra and therefore had to write the various parts so that they could be played on more than one instrument. The contrapuntal style that prevailed from the time of Monteverdi until the mid-18th century usually meant simply assigning instruments to each line in a composition; the basic consideration was whether that line stayed within the range of the chosen instrument. The fixed personnel of such orchestras as the Mannheim group, therefore, freed the composers to experiment with the capabilities of the instruments within the group. Musical style was also changing, the contrapuntal style of the Baroque giving way to a style that relied more heavily on melodic invention supported by harmony.

(CONTINUED ON THE NEXT PAGE)

(CONTINUED FROM THE PREVIOUS PAGE)

One of the more important composers of the period between the Baroque and Classical eras was Johann Sebastian's son, Carl Philipp Emanuel Bach. In C.P.E. Bach's symphonies the strings become melodic instruments, and the winds–two flutes, two oboes, one or two bassoons, two horns–fill out chords and provide body to the orchestration.

The Classical period
The Classical era, which covers roughly the second half of the 18th century, is one of the most significant periods in the development of orchestration. The most talented composers of this period were Mozart and Haydn. Many important developments took place during this time. The orchestra became standardized. The Classical orchestra came to consist of strings (first and second violins, violas, violoncellos, and double basses), two flutes, two oboes, two clarinets, two bassoons, two or four horns, two trumpets, and two timpani. Toward the end of his career, in the *London Symphonies*, Haydn introduced clarinets as part of the woodwind section, a change that was to be permanent. Haydn also introduced the following innovations: trumpets were used independently instead of always doubling the horns, cellos became separated from the double basses, and woodwind instruments were often given the main melodic line. In the *Military Symphony (No. 100)* Haydn introduced some

percussion instruments not normally used in the orchestras of this time, namely, triangle, hand cymbals, and bass drum; and, what is still more unusual, they are employed in the second movement, which in the Classical tradition is normally the slow movement.

In Haydn's music a method of composition appeared that had a bearing on orchestration. This consisted of the conscious use of musical motives; motive is defined in the *Harvard Dictionary of Music* as: "The briefest intelligible and self-contained fragment of a musical theme or subject." Perhaps the best known musical motive in Western music is the four-note group with which Beethoven's *Fifth Symphony* begins. These musical cells became the musical building blocks of the Classical period, particularly in the middle or development section of a movement, with the composer moving the musical motive from instrument to instrument and section to section, giving a new facet to the orchestration. The art of orchestration was thus becoming a major factor in the artistic quality of the music.

Mozart, too, was responsible for great strides in the creative use of instruments. His last two symphonies (Nos. 40, K 550, and 41, K 551) are among the most beautifully orchestrated works of this or any period. For his 17 piano concertos, Mozart exhaustively explored the combination of piano and orchestra.

(CONTINUED ON THE NEXT PAGE)

(CONTINUED FROM THE PREVIOUS PAGE)

The Romantic period

Beethoven began his career under the influence of the Classical composers, particularly Haydn, but during his lifetime he transformed this heritage into the foundation of a new musical practice that was to become known as Romanticism. The Classical composers for the most part attempted to orchestrate with a sense of grace and beauty. Beethoven occasionally made deliberate use of new, intense, often even harsh orchestral sounds. He also, in his later symphonies, augmented the orchestra with a piccolo, contrabassoon, and third and fourth horn. *The Ninth Symphony* has one passage calling for triangle, cymbals, and bass drum, a combination identified with the imitations of Turkish Janissary music in vogue in previous years.

The Romantic era was characterized by great strides in the art of instrumentation, and, in fact, the use of instrumental colour became one of the most salient features of this music. The piano really came into its own as a source of interesting sonorities; the orchestra expanded in size and scope; new instruments were added; and old instruments were improved and made more versatile. The Romantic period saw the appearance of the first textbook on the subject of orchestration. It was the French composer Hector Berlioz's *Traité d'instrumentation et d'orchestration modernes* (1844; *Treatise on Instrumentation and Orchestration*, 1856). Berlioz was one of the most individual orchestrators in the history of music, and his *Symphonie fantastique* (1830) is one of the most remarkable pieces of music to come out of this era. Berlioz made use of colour to depict or suggest events in his music, which was frequently programmatic in character. He called on large forces to express his musical ideas, an idea that persisted throughout the 19th century and into the 20th. Berlioz's *Grande Messe des morts* (*Requiem*, 1837) calls for four flutes, two oboes, two English horns, four clarinets, 12 horns, eight bassoons, 25 first violins, 25 second violins, 20 violas, 20 violoncellos, 18 double basses, eight pairs of timpani, four tam-tams (a type of gong), bass drum, and 10 pairs of cymbals; four brass choirs placed in various parts of the hall, each consisting of four trumpets, four trombones, two tubas, and four ophicleides (a large, now obsolete brass instrument); and a chorus of 80 sopranos, 80 altos, 60 tenors, and 70 basses.

The colouristic ideas in Berlioz's music were carried on in various ways by other important 19th-century composers and reached a culmination in the music of the German composer Richard Strauss and the Austrian Gustav Mahler–both of whom demanded a virtuoso orchestra–and were orchestrated in a complex fashion, although Mahler was capable of very delicate effects.

(CONTINUED ON THE NEXT PAGE)

(CONTINUED FROM THE PREVIOUS PAGE)

Post-Romanticism

Claude Debussy in France was probably the most important composer of the period from 1880 until the turn of the 20th century. The composers of this era attempted to describe scenes and evoke moods by the use of rich harmonies and a wide palette of timbre. No composer ever handled the colours of the orchestra with greater subtlety. Naturally, this is also dependent on his use of harmony, melody, and rhythm, but the dominant impression of a Debussy work is focused on his use of orchestral instruments to create light and shadows. Works that exemplify his techniques are *Prélude à l'après-midi d'un faune* (*Prelude to the Afternoon of a Faun*; 1894), *Nocturnes* (1899), and *La Mer* (*The Sea*; 1905). In *Nocturnes* he uses a wordless women's chorus as a section of the orchestra, functioning as another source of timbre rather than as the transmitter of a text.

Many of the composers who followed Debussy and Mahler brought about radical changes in the use of the orchestra. A good example of some of these changes is in *The Rite of Spring* (1913), by the Russian-born composer Igor Stravinsky. The strings frequently do not assume a dominant role but, rather, often play music that is subservient to the brass or woodwinds. Percussion instruments greatly increased in importance and have continued to do so. In 1931, Edgard Varèse composed an important work, *Ionisation*, for 13 percussion players, a landmark in the emergence of percussion instruments as equal partners in music.

The period between World War I and World War II was dominated by two main schools of composers with vastly differing results for orchestration. One was responsible for the Neoclassical style; the other, gathered around the Austrian composer Arnold Schoenberg, drew heavily on the Romantic movement for its direction. The Neoclassical composers sought to free music from the influence of Impressionism. Whereas the Romantic composers had frequently employed the instrumental forces at hand to create a deliberate sense of vagueness, the Neoclassical composers, beginning in about 1917 with a group in France known as Les Six, attempted to recreate the clarity of the Classical period by turning to models found in the popular music of the period, the music of the dance halls and cabarets. The Neoclassical composers also turned away somewhat from the orchestra as a medium, finding the forces of chamber music more suitable for their ideals. Neoclassical music returned to a clearer concept of "sections" in orchestration. The music of a composer such as Paul Hindemith

(CONTINUED ON THE NEXT PAGE)

(CONTINUED FROM THE PREVIOUS PAGE)

in Germany is closer to the music of Mozart in its sense of instrumentation than it is to Romanticism.

The music of Schoenberg and his fellow Austrian Alban Berg drew heavily on the Romantic movement and eventually became known as Expressionism, which stressed inner experience. Emphasis on the inner self produced a music that was thick, dark, and intense.

In the first half of the 20th century electronic music emerged, although it did not become important until after 1950. The principal reasons for the inclusion here of electronic music are that electronic sounds, either taped or live, frequently are included in a composition combined with traditional instruments, and it has had a decided influence on orchestration. By the 1960s many composers were writing works for electronic sounds and instruments. The electronic sounds provide a dimension to instrumentation never before possible. A number of things are noteworthy. Electronic sounds are capable of incredibly subtle changes of timbre, pitch, and mode of attack. When combined with traditional instruments they add a rich new spectrum of colour. This in turn has influenced the composer to attempt to produce "electronic" sounds with standard instruments. The result has been a great extension of the sound possibilities of Western instruments.

Digital technology, with which sound waves can be converted into binary ones and zeros that a computer can process, has rapidly accelerated progress in electronic composition since the turn of this century. Until recently, the equipment required to work with electronic sounds was expensive and bulky. Today, compositions of astonishing diversity and quality are rendered daily on tablet computers.

Another 20th-century trend was away from large orchestras and toward chamber ensembles, often of nontraditional combinations. Compositions for such ensembles often excelled in economy of means and explored individual instrumental timbres.

Arrangement and transcription

A practice that was much employed in the 20th century, although by no means confined to it, was the writing of arrangements and transcriptions. Though little distinction was made between the two, there were differences. A transcription is essentially the adaptation of a composition for an instrument or instruments other than those for which it was originally written. An arrangement is a similar procedure, although the arranger often feels free to take musical liberties with elements of the original score. This is especially true of arrangements for jazz or rock groups and arrangements of popular compositions or songs from musical comedies.

(CONTINUED ON THE NEXT PAGE)

(CONTINUED FROM THE PREVIOUS PAGE)

In the 18th and 19th centuries, chamber and orchestral music was transcribed, or "arranged," for the piano for the purpose of study and, of course, for the pleasure of playing at home the music that had been heard at a concert. This practice has continued into the 21st century. Piano versions of many 18th- and 19th-century orchestral works exist in two- and four-hand arrangements. Another common practice is to reduce the orchestral parts of concertos to a keyboard version to enable students to study and play these works without an orchestra.

The symphonic band, despite its popularity in Great Britain and North America, was faced with a dearth of repertoire written specifically for it. In the past, one answer was to transcribe orchestral works for band, substituting particularly the clarinets, with their wide pitch range, for the strings of the symphony orchestra. The necessity for that substitution is no longer so great because in recent times composers have written much more music specifically for the symphonic band.

The dance band predominant in the 1930s and 1940s is treated roughly in the following way by arrangers: the saxophones carry the melody more frequently than the other sections; the trumpets provide embellishment or figures that work around the melody; the trombones either are combined with the trumpets or serve as a melodic instrument; the piano and guitar provide harmonic filler; and the double bass and drums set the rhythm.

The jazz or rock arranger has done much more than simply transcribe the keyboard version of a song. All forms of popular music in the 20th and 21st centuries have been involved in the art of improvising. Musicians working in this field almost always embellish the music as they perform it. The jazz or rock arranger in a sense improvises on manuscript paper. In making an arrangement for a group of musicians the arranger will embellish both the harmonic structure and the melody of the composition; or the arrangement will be worked out in rehearsal and memorized or written down later. Usually, the arranger keeps enough of the original material to enable the listener to recognize the source. His skill depends on how well he can manipulate the materials of the original and on his originality in scoring the composition for the group at his disposal. The men and women who work in this field are frequently composers of popular music themselves.

THE 20TH CENTURY AND EARLY 21ST CENTURY

Richard Wagner's highly expressive harmonic bequest could not but drive chromaticism eventually beyond the retaining confines of the idea of a central key, for the extensive use of chromatic chords tends to blur the listener's ability to perceive the basic harmonic relationships that define a key. In their nontonal compositional procedures, Arnold Schoenberg and his 20th-century Second Viennese school abandoned the concept of key, using all notes freely without relating them to the system of functional harmony. They thus represent not so much a reaction to as a logical extension of Wagnerian principles. Wagner's compelling artistic personality certainly exercised near-magic powers over many of his younger contemporaries and successors, exceeding even Beethoven's spell. But others, too, contributed to "the music of the future." As Schoenberg was to point out in one of his remarkable essays, even Brahms, who looked upon himself as a conservative in the best sense of the term, was, historically speaking, a true "progressive," especially in his propensity for irregular phrasing and complex motivic manipulations.

The growth of political nationalism in the "peripheral" countries of Europe also had significant repercussions in musical composition. In the last half of the 19th century distinctive folk-music elements, previously totally unheeded by Europe's elitist musical cultures, found enthusiastic response in sophisticated circles, exerting an "exotic" attraction similar to that which had accounted earlier in the century for the Romantic infatuation with Eastern civilizations. Thus at a time when the exhaustion of Europe's "civilized" compositional resources appeared imminent, the "untutored" harmonies of the Russian composer Modest Mussorgsky—steeped in the spirit of Russian folk music and based on chord progressions alien to the standard harmonic usage of his day—helped breathe new life into a harmonic language about to succumb to redundant overdoses of functional chromaticism. Mussorgsky thus paved the way for the later whole-tone and pentatonic (five-note scale) experiments of Claude Debussy and Béla Bartók.

What was being questioned publicly in many quarters at the dawn of the 20th century was the evolutionistic view of Western art music as man's ultimate achievement in the realm of sound and its logical consequent that 19th-century harmony represented in turn music's most advanced stage of development. This increasing skepticism, given by the nature of late 19th-century music itself, was strongly reinforced by the growing awareness of historical compositional techniques that resulted from the mushrooming discoveries of musicological scholarship. Before long, all manner of pre-19th-century textures and structural principles were seized upon to counteract the type of self-defeating post-Wagnerianism—so tragically exemplified in several of the most ambitious works of Max Reger. The 20th-century search for fresh, flexible techniques extended far beyond the nontonal Second Viennese school of Schoenberg. In historical perspective, Anton Webern's fascination with 15th-century canonic techniques, Paul Hindemith's predilection for both modal and early-18th-century polyphony, Igor Stravinsky's emulation of Domenico Scarlatti, and, for that matter, Kurt Weill's reinterpretation of John Gay's *Beggar's Opera* (1728) represent but various individual and culturally conditioned manifestations of the same determination: to put the burden of history to positive use in a concerted effort to revitalize an art that seemed moribund by the time World War I changed the socio-economic and political physiognomy of Europe.

Historically, Schoenberg's formulation of the laws of composition with 12 tones—involving the consistent melodic and harmonic use of a specifically arranged sequence of the 12 notes of the chromatic scale—sprang in the early 1920s from the same obsession with textural and structural clarity that marked the postwar Neoclassical syndrome as a whole. Schoenberg himself may have considered his most fundamental contribution to musical history to be "the emancipation of dissonance"—a relativistic conception of intervals and chords that disregarded the careful regulation of dissonance characteristic of functional harmony. Actually, the 12-tone procedures he developed so consistently served to restore, to an extent far beyond that which Mahler had been able to achieve within the traditional harmonic framework, the primacy of motivic-contrapuntal development as a musical resource. Thus it was that the profusion of simultaneous melodies that animates Mahler's *Symphony No. 4 in G Major* (completed 1900) found its ultimate potential realized in Schoenberg's most uncompromising polyphonic work, the *Wind Quintet* (1924).

Possibly the most successful attempt to regenerate Beethovenian procedures without the total abandonment of functional tonality is represented by the string quartets and certain other instrumental compositions of Bartók. Drawing upon the rhythmic-melodic properties of Hungarian and Romanian folk music, Bartók produced a unique type of functionally extended harmony determined largely by the contrapuntal inter-action of motives. Others, such as Charles Ives in the United States and, under the impact of South American popular music, Darius Milhaud in France, transcended traditional tonality by writing polytonally (in two or three keys simultaneously).

Whatever their specific approach, progressive 20th-century composers everywhere clearly gave precedence to melodic-rhythmic energies. Even instrumental colour was pressed into the service of melodic definition. Years before World War I Schoenberg had advocated in practice (*Five Orchestral Pieces*) and in theory (*Harmonielehre*, 1911; *Theory of Harmony*, 1947 [the English edition omits the pertinent chapter]) the idea of tone-colour melody, or *Klangfarbenmelodie*. But it was his pupil Webern who, in his mature works, divided the individual components of melodic phrases over several instruments as an imaginatively colouristic reinforce-ment of the complex polyphony that characterized his style. After World War II Webern's procedures were adopted enthusiastically by composers on both sides of the Atlantic. Living in increasingly automated societ-ies, the post-Webern composers soon discovered total serialism, a manner of composition in which all musi-cal parameters follow numerical rules laid down in the course of what has been called the precompositional process. Whereas Schoenberg's row technique merely fixed the sequence of the 12 pitches of the chromatic scale in accordance with the motivic context of a given piece, Webern had indeed begun to serialize rhythm and to some extent instrumentation, possibly under the influence of medieval isorhythmic techniques. But total serialization, as practiced by the post-Webernians, left little, if anything, to spontaneous inspiration, and the

1950s thus witnessed the closing of a creative circle initiated during the early Middle Ages when spontaneous inspiration was manifestly suspect. Perhaps inevitably, such a hermetically closed system of composition provoked reactions that moved the aesthetic pendulum violently to the extreme opposite position. Spur-of-the-moment action became the watchword in music as well as in life generally. Aleatory (chance-music) composition in its more radical manifestations provides only minimal guidelines for performers who are told to improvise freely within certain temporal or spatial limitations, or both.

Thus, in the first quarter of the 21st century, the West has returned, insofar as is possible, to the pre-typographical stage when musical tradition was essentially oral. More than that, the relatively recent replacement of "the public," once essentially the cultural elite, by a whole host of publics to whom mutually exclusive types of composers cater with great solicitude, suggests that the private musical life of the immediate past is in the process of being transplanted by experiences serving, among other things, the identification of special group interests and needs. At the same time, novelty rather than originality has become the order of the day. Musical compositions, electronically recorded—more recently also electronically produced—and distributed as salable items by mass-oriented corporations, have attained the status of physical objects that are easily discarded and replaced. Still, there are those who try to transform the burdens of history into significant new forms of composition. A new eclecticism is in the making, destined perhaps to preserve a long tradition that has been among the West's proudest achievements.

Recording studios began using equipment to digitize music in the late 20th century. Digitization made it possible for people to listen to music on the Internet and to download and share music files, using their computers and mobile devices such as smart phones. This radically has changed the way consumers access music.

For composers, music notation software makes it very easy to create elaborate compositions using only a computer. One result has been an explosion in musical compositions as in other forms of art. Advanced programs enable composers to duplicate the sounds produced by conventional instruments with amazing accuracy. Composers also can experiment with timbres and tones to produce new sounds that cannot be mimicked by any known instrument.

MUSICAL FORM

J ust as buildings and bridges have architectural designs and shapes, magazines have thoughtful and attractive layouts, and art masterpieces begin with conceptual sketches, music, too, is created by design. It does not come into being spontaneously. It is constructed using existing structures of sound.

Musical form is the framework of a musical composition. The term is regularly used in two senses: to denote a standard type, or genre, and to denote the procedures in a specific work. The nomenclature for the various musical formal types may be determined by the medium of performance, the technique of composition, or by function.

PRINCIPLES OF MUSICAL FORM

Music exists in time; as philosopher Susanne K. Langer phrased it in *Feeling and Form*, "music is time made audible." The proper perception of a musical work depends in the main on the ability to associate what is happening in the present with what has happened in the past and with what one expects will happen in the future. The frustration or fulfillment of such expectations and the resulting tensions and releases are basic to most musical works.

Musical form depends, therefore, on the disposition of certain structural units successively in time. The basic principles can be discerned from a brief consideration of melody, which may be defined as an organized succession of musical tones. This succession of tones consists of component parts, structural units, the principal of which is the phrase—a complete musical utterance, roughly corresponding to what can be sung or played in one breath or played with a single stroke of the bow. A melody, then, ordinarily consists of a succession of phrases, in which there may occur repetition (the same phrase repeated), contrast (a completely different phrase), or variation (the phrase altered, but in such a way that its identity remains perceptible). The relation between these component phrases is important for form. There may, for instance, be a complementary grouping of phrases as antecedent and consequent or "question and answer." The phrases may or may not be equal in length. Some writers, pressing the analogy between music and language, also distinguish larger groupings of phrases: into periods, sentences, paragraphs, and the like. Most musical forms are thus not only additive but also hierarchical: phrases are conjoined to produce a melody, which in turn may be a constituent part of a larger work. A melodic entity that functions as an element in a larger whole is called a theme.

Coherence may be produced by the use of a motive or figure, i.e., short elements consisting ordinarily of two to four notes. But whereas the motive is usually characterized by a striking interval or rhythmic arrangement, the figure consists of entirely conventional elements (a scale segment, notes of a chord, etc.). Finally, coherence may also be achieved by the consistent use of a rhythmic pattern.

A few examples will serve to illustrate these points. The various phrases have been identified by slurs (phrase marks) and by lowercase letters (the exponential numbers designate variations), whereas larger groupings are designated by capital letters. In the hymn tune "Bethany," by Lowell Mason, shown below, the eight phrases may be grouped in pairs to produce the scheme:

$$a\ b \qquad a\ b^1 \qquad c\ c^1 \qquad a\ b^1$$
$$A \qquad\quad A^1 \qquad\quad B \qquad\quad A^1$$

This four-phase arrangement with statement, repetition (here with variation at the cadence), contrast, and restatement is extremely common in the traditional and art music of the West.

Other schemes based on repetition and contrast abound. The famous "Largo" from Antonín Dvořák's *New World Symphony*, Opus 95, goes like this:

Here the scheme is:

a a¹   b b   a a²
A   B   A¹

This common arrangement is known as three-part form. Coherence is provided by the use of a rhythmic motive,

(marked "x" in the second example).

A common device is melodic sequence, in which the phrase is repeated but in transposition, as in the refrain of the Christmas carol "O Come All Ye Faithful."

O come let us a–dore him, O

come let us a – dore him

Different from the above procedures is an English traditional song, "How Should I Your True Love Know" (example follows). The phrase structure here is a b c d, so that there is no repetitive plan. Such a melody is said to be through-composed. In some through-composed melodies a rhythmic pattern may appear throughout to promote coherence.

Other elements contribute to formal organization in music. Among those having solely to do with pitch are range or register—whether most of the activity is high, low, or in the middle, or combinations of these, and whether the range of pitches used is large or small; types of melodic motion,

whether conjunct (i.e., by step along the scale) or disjunct (by leaps); and the use of different types of scales or modes. Factors included in music's temporal aspect include tempo, whether fast or slow, as well as duration; i.e., whether individual notes are long or short (the gradually increasing use of constantly shorter note values, for instance, is associated with acceleration and accumulation, thus with increasing intensity). Among the harmonic aspects, there is key, or tonality (set of interrelated notes and chords, based on a major or minor scale), whereby the reassertion of a key following the intervention of other keys may produce an effect akin to the restatement of a phrase after a contrasting one has been heard; in this respect, cadences (sections giving the impression of conclusion) are of crucial importance in defining key. Still other factors include the use of dynamics (loud and soft); timbre, or tone colour, especially in the employment of unusual instruments or combinations of instruments; texture, whether monophonic (consisting of a single melodic line) or polyphonic (many-voiced), be it contrapuntal (having simultaneous independent melodic lines) or homophonic (one voice leading melodically, supported by chordal procedures); and, in vocal music, whether the text is set syllabically (one note to a syllable) or melismatically (many notes to a syllable).

FORMAL TYPES

Four basic types of musical forms are distinguished in ethnomusicology: iterative, the same phrase repeated over and over; reverting, with the restatement of a phrase after a contrasting one; strophic, a larger melodic entity repeated over and over to different strophes (stanzas) of a poetic text; and progressive, in which new melodic material is continuously presented (thus synonymous with through-composed). The following discussion deals first with Western and then with non-Western music.

ITERATIVE AND REVERTING TYPES

Iterative types, not common in Western music, may be found in the recitation tones of Gregorian chant, in which, for example, each line of a psalm is sung to the same melodic formula. Far more common, however, are reverting types. In the Middle Ages there existed the fixed forms used in songs, such as the French ballade (a a b), virelai (A b b a A), and rondeau (A B a A a b A B), the Italian ballata (A b b a A) and the German bar form (a a b), where the patterns of repetition and contrast correspond to poetic forms. (In the representations of the reverting types in songs, lowercase letters refer to the same music set to different words, while capital letters indicate that both text and music are the same.) Since the Baroque period (c. 1600–c. 1750) there has been binary, or two-part form, such as a b. A variety of binary form particularly prominent in the dances of the 18th century is the rounded binary form, the two sections of which are a and b a (i.e., with a final return to original material in the second section), each of which is repeated, part one being heard twice before part two begins: ‖: a :‖ ‖: b a :‖ (‖: and :‖ indicate the enclosed material is to be repeated).

BINARY

The rounded binary form took on great importance in the late 18th century, when it was expanded and elaborated into what is known as sonata form (also called sonata-allegro or first movement form), which may be represented thus: ‖: exposition :‖ ‖: development recapitulation :‖, whereby the kinship to the ‖: a :‖ ‖: b a:‖ structure of rounded binary form is clear. Ordinarily, in the exposition the principal musical themes are stated; in the development they are subjected to a process of working out and variation; and, finally, in the recapitulation they are restated. Sometimes the scheme is enlarged by adding a slow introduction before the exposition or a coda (concluding passage) at the end, or both. This formal principle, usually treated with a certain freedom, has been of basic importance in Western instrumental music since the mid-18th century.

TERNARY

Another basic reverting type is ternary (three-part) form, a b a, also known as "song form" because of its frequent use in that genre, as well as in character pieces for piano. The form dominates the aria in late Baroque opera (the da capo aria, in which the final statement of a is not written out, but the performers simply follow the written instruction da capo, meaning "from the beginning," and repeat the first part). The da capo principle also appears in the instrumental minuet and scherzo with trio.

RONDO

On a larger scale are refrain schemes, in which contrasting episodes appear between statements of the refrain. In instrumental music this is found most often in a five-part arrangement, the rondo, frequently a b a c a b a; but many departures from the form occur, most common being the replacement of c by a development passage, usually based on the rondo theme. This important variant, known as the sonata-rondo, is particularly associated with Joseph Haydn. The refrain principle also appears in the rondeau of 18th-century French harpsichord music, in which there is no set limit to the number of episodes. The third movements of concertos, with the reversions of the tutti or ritornello (passage for full orchestra) and the intervening episodes for the solo instrument or instruments, are also of this type, as occasionally are large operatic arias.

STROPHIC TYPES

The strophic type is seen in hymns and traditional ballads, in which different poetic strophes are set to the same melody. Thus, while the melody of a single stanza may accord with one of the reverting types, the hymn or ballad as a whole is strophic; this also applies to the fixed forms of medieval music and to many other types of song, simple and complex.

The instrumental equivalent of the strophic type is variation (or theme and variation) form, in which a musical theme, often a complete melody with a harmonic accompaniment, is stated and then repeated a number of times, but with variations. A clear example of the relation between variation and strophic form is the chorale-partita of the Baroque era, a keyboard piece based on a hymn, with each varied statement of the hymn tune corresponding to a strophe of the hymn text. But the structure is more common in independent instrumental compositions, often of considerable dimensions (e.g., Beethoven's *Diabelli Variations* for piano). In the Baroque a common type was the ostinato, or variations on a ground, in which the composition was built on a recurring melodic or harmonic pattern, generally in the bass, the accompanying parts being varied with each statement of the pattern, as in Bach's *Passacaglia and Fugue in C Minor* for organ or his "Chaconne" from the *Partita in D Minor* for unaccompanied violin. This procedure is also found in early operatic arias in the strophic variation form, in which each statement of the ostinato corresponds to a strophe of the aria's text. In the 19th century Brahms made impressive use of the ostinato (finales of the *Variations on a Theme by Haydn* and the *Symphony No. 4 in E Minor*).

PROGRESSIVE TYPES

The progressive type is common in songs and instrumental pieces of the 19th and 20th centuries, but is also found in earlier music (e.g., in the melodies used for the Gloria and Credo of the mass in plainchant) and in the prose, or sequence (c. 9th–c. 12th centuries), the phrases of which are arranged in pairs (a a b b c c d d, etc.), and its instrumental equivalent, the estampie. Polyphonic forms using a cantus firmus or basic melody (often a plainchant excerpt) also belong to the progressive type and include the liturgical organum, the early motet, and the conductus from the medieval era, as well as many chorale-preludes for organ of the Baroque. If, however, the cantus firmus itself is in one of the reverting forms, then the polyphonic setting will frequently follow suit.

The most important forms of Renaissance polyphony also belong to the progressive type, since the characteristic procedure was to give each line of the text its own musical phrase, as in the Renaissance motet and other types of secular polyphonic music. The same applies to the instrumental contrapuntal forms of the late Renaissance and Baroque: the ricercare, canzona, invention, and fugue. Other progressive types include intonations, preludes, toccatas, and fantasias for lute and keyboard of the 16th, 17th, and early 18th centuries, in which the thematic material consists primarily of figurative elements (scale passages, arpeggiated chords, trills, turns, and the like); in larger works of this kind—by Bach for instance—passages in fugal style are often also present. Finally, there is simple binary form (a b), often found in early dances and in large operatic arias of the Classical period (Mozart and Beethoven).

WESTERN COMPOUND FORMS

With the larger forms of instrumental music there are extended musical pieces, usually called movements, which in their succession and totality make up a larger whole. An important unifying factor is key: a single key often dominates the work, others being used for contrast. This idea goes back at least to the Baroque, when two formal types were established: the first is the *sonata da camera*, or chamber sonata, consisting of a series of dances in the same key (also known as partita and, later, suite). By J.S. Bach's time (1685–1750) a set arrangement of dances was common: allemande (moderate duple time), courante or corrente (fast triple time), saraband (slow triple time), and gigue (fast duple or quadruple time), usually with some other dance inserted between the saraband and the gigue. The other type is the *sonata da chiesa*, or church sonata, which consists of four movements, again all in the same key, in a slow–fast–slow–fast succession. The distinction between the two types is explicit in Bach's sonatas and partitas for unaccompanied violin: the sonatas are in the "church" form, whereas the partitas are suites. Other large forms of Baroque music are the two types of overture: the French, in two parts, the first slow and stately, the second fast and fugal; and the Italian, in three movements in the succession fast–slow–fast, the middle movement usually in a different key. The instrumental concerto after 1700 usually employed the same scheme as the Italian overture.

THE SONATA

Around 1750 a combination of these types produced the forms most common in the standard repertory of concert music. The sonata became a piece for either a keyboard instrument or a solo instrument accompanied by keyboard. It ordinarily consisted either of three movements in the arrangement fast–slow–fast or of four, with a minuet inserted between the slow movement and the finale; but there are examples of two-movement sonatas, notably by Beethoven, and even of one-movement sonatas (e.g., by Domenico Scarlatti, the Italian-born composer to the Spanish court). Usually all movements except the slow one (and sometimes the trio, as well) are in the same key. The first movement typically is cast in the sonata form, the slow movement in one of the reverting schemes (often ternary), and the finale either in sonata or rondo form; but variation form may appear in any of these movements.

This large form is also used in chamber music, particularly the string quartet, and in the large form of orchestral music, the symphony, both of which ordinarily have four movements. Notable exceptions to this are the late quartets of Beethoven as well as those of the 20th-century composer Béla Bartók, the latter in two instances using what is called the "arch form," a large reverting arrangement, A B C B A, each element being a separate movement; there are innumerable other exceptions. The concerto, on the other hand, adheres more to the older three-movement form. The various kinds of late 18th-century entertainment music (cassation, divertimento, nocturne, serenade, and the like) may employ any of a number of arrangements, ranging from three movements all the way to six or more.

CYCLIC FORM

Some authorities believe that since the 18th century such sonata-form compositions have been organized by the use of a few musical thematic motives, often submitted to considerable variation throughout. Compositions organized in such a way are said to be in cyclic form. While this becomes important in the 19th century, the extent to which it characterizes the Classical period is a matter of some controversy at present.

FANTASIAS AND PROGRAM MUSIC

Simultaneously a much freer form was cultivated, beginning in the late 18th century, the fantasia, primarily for keyboard, notably in the hands of Carl Philipp Emanuel Bach. Consisting of an indefinite number of highly contrasting sections, surprise and expression were of prime significance.

The fantasia, along with the overture to a play or opera, was the precursor of the large forms of orchestral program music of the 19th century, in which an extramusical content (usually a narrative of some kind), called the program, is expressed in the composition. There are two main types: the program symphony, associated with Hector Berlioz, in which the norms of symphonic form are for the most part preserved, and the symphonic poem, associated with Franz Liszt and Richard Strauss, in which the composer allows the extramusical subject matter to determine the structure of the composition. Some 19th-century concert overtures by German composers such as Felix Mendelssohn and Robert Schumann belong to this type of composition. Important here is the association of musical themes with aspects of the program, the themes being used throughout the work, often in varied forms.

Another arrangement is called the suite, which no longer consists exclusively of dances but also of instrumental pieces of all kinds. Usually some common element runs throughout: a cyclic theme may be used, as in Schumann's *Carnaval* or the Russian composer Modest Mussorgsky's *Pictures from an Exhibition*, or the

FANTASIA

Fantasia, also called fantasy or fancy, is a composition free in form and inspiration, usually for an instrumental soloist; in 16th- and 17th-century England the term was applied especially to fugal compositions (i.e., based on melodic imitation) for consorts of string or wind instruments. Earlier 16th-century fantasias for lute or keyboard consisted of short sections based on one or more musical motives. In England the fantasy or fancy for keyboard, lute, or viola had a late flowering at the time of Henry Purcell (1659–95).

In the 17th and early 18th centuries in Germany the organ *Fantasie* reflected this improvisatory character, in direct contrast to the highly structured fugue that usually followed. Freedom of form and execution persisted in the fantasias of Carl Philipp Emanuel Bach (1714–88), Mozart, Beethoven, and Franz Schubert, some of which retained the fugal element as well. Robert Schumann in his *Fantasie, Opus 17* (1836), and Frédéric Chopin in his *Fantaisie in F Minor* (1840) maintained the tradition of a single, self-contained movement, at least outwardly. But later works, including Arnold Schoenberg's *Phantasy for Violin and Piano* (1949), frequently recall the sectionalized arrangement that prevailed during the Renaissance and early Baroque periods. The complex contrapuntal keyboard fantasias of J.S. Bach (e.g., *Chromatic Fantasy and Fugue*, c. 1720), on the other hand, inspired similar works by Franz Liszt, Max Reger, and Ferruccio Busoni. Some composers have exploited the fantasia for its programmatic, or descriptive, possibilities, among them John Mundy (died 1630), who wrote a fantasia on the weather, and Pyotr Ilyich Tchaikovsky, who composed his symphonic fantasy *Francesca da Rimini* in 1876. While appealing particularly to the romantic imagination, the fantasia served, from the beginning, also as a vehicle for instrumental elaboration of vocal music (e.g., Schubert's "Wanderer" fantasy [1822], based on one of his own songs, and Ralph Vaughan Williams's *Fantasia on "Greensleeves"* [1934]).

music may originally have been intended for use with a play (Mendelssohn's music to *A Midsummer Night's Dream* or the Norwegian Edvard Grieg's for Henrik Ibsen's *Peer Gynt*).

OPERA AND ORATORIO

Among the large forms of vocal music, opera and oratorio are the most significant. Both are extended works in which a narrative is set to music. While an opera is performed in a theatre, an oratorio is a concert piece. Both may be either sacred or secular. A special type of oratorio is the Passion, the setting of New Testament accounts of Christ's crucifixion. The cantata may be regarded as a smaller form of oratorio.

Operas and oratorios ordinarily consist of several musical genres: recitative (imitating the manner of speech), aria, ensemble and choral pieces, often with instrumental interludes and an overture (most overtures of the late 18th and 19th centuries being cast in sonata form). Opera often includes ballets and large sectional finales at the ends of acts. With respect to the oratorio, Handel greatly increased the role of the chorus in his work with this genre (especially *Israel in Egypt* [1739]), an example seized upon by his successors. Oratorios also differ from operas in that they frequently make use of a testo (narrator), who relates the events of the action, usually set in recitative style. Stravinsky's *Oedipus Rex* (1927) combines the two traditions.

Whereas operas are usually composed as a series of enclosed musical forms, the German composer Richard Wagner devised a special kind, known as music drama, in which the music is continuous and in which the distinction between recitative, aria, and ensemble

Anthony Dean Griffey (*left*) and Waltraud Meier (*middle*) perform Igor Stravinsky's *Oedipus Rex*, which combines opera and oratorio, with the New York Philharmonic, conducted by Varely Gergiev (*right*), at Avery Fisher Hall.

is largely eliminated. Instead, Wagner used a flexible melodic line which he referred to as "tone speech." Wagner also greatly increased the role of the orchestra, stressing the technique of thematic development and transformation borrowed from instrumental music and further associating each theme with an aspect of the operatic plot, such themes being known as leitmotivs ("leading motifs").

THE MASS

Another large vocal form is the mass, the earliest polyphonic settings of which date from the 14th century.

At first the mass was set in cantus firmus style, each movement built on the appropriate Gregorian chant melody, as in the mass of the French composer Guillaume de Machaut. In the 15th century a Burgundian composer, Guillaume Dufay, and his contemporaries developed the cyclic mass, in which a single cantus firmus was employed throughout. This idea was extended in the parody mass, built by elaborating thematic material taken from an existing polyphonic work, usually a motet or chanson; most 16th-century masses are of this kind. In the Baroque mass, each segment of the text is treated as an independent composition (aria, duet, chorus), similar to the procedure in a cantata or oratorio, except that no recitatives are used. J.S. Bach's *Mass in B Minor* (1733) is of this type.

In the 16th and 17th centuries, Monteverdi and others grouped madrigals into a kind of cycle around a particular subject; should a dramatic text be involved, the form is known as a madrigal comedy. In the 19th century and after, similarly grouped songs with piano accompaniment are known as a song cycle (e.g., those by Beethoven, Schubert, and Schumann).

20TH-CENTURY MODIFICATIONS AND BEYOND

In the 20th century many composers continued to use the traditional forms, although in other respects their work made significant departures from what had been established. Others virtually discarded them. Radically new elements were introduced to serve as structural units: instead of the traditional phrases and motives, composers came to employ what they call "sound events," combinations of textures, types of timbre, aggregates of different simultaneously sounding pitches, and the like. An early example is afforded by the notion of the melody of timbres—the *Klangfarbenmelodie* of Arnold Schoenberg and Anton von Webern. The broadest possible range is included in the conception of a sound event: not merely tones but also noises; in fact, sounds of all kinds. These sound events have been arranged in a complex manner. An important principle of organization has been serialism, originally applied only to pitch, so that the pitch content of the work is decided by reiterations of a series (set or row) of pitches that has been determined in advance (e.g., in the 12-tone compositions of Schoenberg and Webern). Since 1945 the serial principle has been extended to other aspects of music as well: durations, dynamics, and types of attack and tempi, as in the music of the French composer Olivier Messiaen and the German Karlheinz Stockhausen. Other composers, including Stockhausen and the Greek Yannis Xenakis, have used numerical relationships to determine the structure of compositions mathematically. Still others have conceived of form as a dynamic interaction between contrasting and continually evolving sound events—the French composer Edgard Varèse and the American Elliott Carter. Simultaneously, there are works, such as those of the American John Cage, in which the form is not predetermined by the composer but left to chance, such pieces being called indeterminate or aleatory. These statements apply particularly to electronic music.

By and large, composers in the 21st century feel encouraged to explore their individuality in musical form. Emerging works are increasingly diverse and provocative. The multitude of 21st-century composers worthy of study include John Adams, Julian Anderson, Anthony Braxton, Brian Ferneyhough, Philip Glass, Michael Nyman, and Julia Wolfe.

MUSICAL INSTRUMENTS

The principal types of musical instruments, classified by the method of producing sound, are percussion, stringed, keyboard, wind, and electronic. Musical instruments are almost universal components of human culture: archaeology has revealed pipes and whistles in the Paleolithic Period and clay drums and shell trumpets in the Neolithic Period. It has been firmly established that the ancient city cultures of Mesopotamia, the Mediterranean, India, East Asia, and the Americas all possessed diverse and well-developed assortments of musical instruments, indicating that a long previous development must have existed. As to the origin of musical instruments, however, there can be only conjecture. Some scholars have speculated that the first instruments were derived from such utilitarian objects as cooking pots (drums) and hunting bows (musical bows); others have argued that instruments of music might well have preceded pots and bows; while in the myths of cultures throughout the world the origin of music has frequently been attributed to the gods, especially in areas where music seems to have been regarded as an essential component of the ritual believed necessary for spiritual survival.

Whatever their origin, the further development of the enormously varied instruments of the world has been dependent on the interplay of four factors: available material, technological skills, mythic and symbolic preoccupations, and patterns of trade and migration. Thus, residents of Arctic regions use bone, skin, and stone to construct instruments; residents of the tropics have wood, bamboo, and reed available; while societies with access to metals and the requisite technology are able to utilize these malleable materials in a variety of ways. Myth and symbolism play an equally important role. Herding societies, for example, which may depend on a particular species of animal not only economically but also spiritually, often develop instruments that look or sound like the animal or prefer instruments made of bone and hide rather than stone and wood, even when all the materials are available. Finally, patterns of human trade and migration have for many centuries swept musicians and their instruments across seas and continents, resulting in constant flux, change, and cross-fertilization and adaptation.

The sound produced by an instrument can be affected by many factors, including the material from which the instrument is made, its size and shape, and the way that it is played. For example, a stringed instrument may be struck, plucked, or bowed, each method producing a distinctive sound. A wooden instrument struck by a beater sounds markedly different from a metal instrument, even if the two instruments are otherwise identical. On the other hand, a flute made of metal does not produce a substantially different sound from one made of wood, for in this case the vibrations are in the column of air in the instrument. The characteristic timbre of wind instruments depends on other factors, notably the length and shape of the tube. The length of the tube not only determines the pitch but also affects the timbre: the piccolo, being half the size of the flute, has a shriller sound. The shape of the tube determines the presence or absence of the "upper partials" (harmonic or nonharmonic overtones), which give colour to the single note.

This chapter discusses the evolution of musical instruments, their structure and methods of sound production, and the purposes for which they have been used. It focuses on the families of instruments that have been prominent in Western art music.

GENERAL CHARACTERISTICS

Musical instruments have been used since earliest times for a variety of purposes, ranging from the entertainment of concert audiences to the accompaniment of dances, rituals, work, and medicine. The use of instruments for religious ceremonies has continued down to the present day, though at various times they have been suspect because of their secular associations. The many references to instruments in the Hebrew Bible (Old Testament) are evidence of the fact that they played an important part in Jewish worship until for doctrinal reasons they were excluded. It is also clear that the early Christians in the eastern Mediterranean used instruments in their services, since the practice was severely condemned by ecclesiastics, who insisted that the references to instruments in the Psalms were to be interpreted symbolically. Although instruments continue to be banned in Islamic mosques (but not in religious processions or Sufi ritual) and in the traditional Eastern

Orthodox church, they play important roles in the ritual of most other societies. For example, Buddhist cultures are rich in instruments, particularly bells and drums (and in the Tibet Autonomous Region of China, wind instruments as well).

Belief in the magical properties of instruments is found in many societies. The Jewish shofar (a ram's horn), which is still blown on Rosh Hashana (New Year) and Yom Kippur (Day of Atonement), must be heard by the congregation. The power of the shofar is illustrated by the story of Joshua at the siege of Jericho: when the priests blew their shofars seven times, the walls of the city fell flat. In India, according to legend, when the deity Krishna played the flute, the rivers stopped flowing and the birds came down to listen. The birds are said to have done the same in 14th-century Italy when the composer Francesco Landini played his *organetto*, or portative organ. In China, instruments were identified with the points of the compass, with the seasons, and with natural phenomena. The Melanesian bamboo flute was a charm for rebirth.

Many of the instruments used in medieval Europe came from western Asia, and they have retained some of their original symbolism. For example, trumpets, long associated with military operations, had a ceremonial function in the establishment of European kings and nobles and were, in fact, regarded as a sign of nobility. In the later Middle Ages and for long afterward, they were associated with kettledrums (known originally as nakers, after their Arab name, *naqqārah*), which were often played on horseback, as they still are in some mounted regiments. Trumpet fanfares, heard on ceremonial occasions in the modern world, are a survival of medieval practice.

TECHNOLOGICAL DEVELOPMENTS

Conventional Western thinking claimed that the earliest instruments were slightly modified natural objects such as bones, shells, or gourds. They played only one pitch and then evolved into more complex forms. However, it appears that bone flutes from Neanderthal caves had finger holes, and recent archaeological finds in China included bone flutes from 7000 BCE that not only have seven finger holes but an additional aperture that may have been drilled to correct a poorly placed hole. Thus, early humans appear to have been just as sensitive to pitch and tone colour as were most other sentient creatures, such as birds, cats, dogs, and whales. None of the sounds they heard or made moved from simple to complex. Aztec clay versions of shell trumpets imitated the internal chambers of the nautilus; the instruments' construction may indicate a sophisticated use of the overtone series to obtain varied pitches (as is done on the bugle).

The stretched string of a bow can produce several pitches when it is beaten, and the string can be stopped at points along its length to produce varied sounds. In addition, a resonator such as a pot or gourd is often used to increase the volume of the sound. The player's mouth can add variety to both volume and pitch. A tube of bamboo can become musical when it is struck on the ground, and a set of different-sized tubes can produce a melodic and rhythmic ensemble. Lifting strips of the bark from a tube and adding bridges under the strips creates a melodic zither, for which each strip produces a separate pitch. The sound can be enhanced by placing one end of the tube in a resonator, whether a gourd or a

Luthier Roberto Caretti works on a guitar in his workshop near Turin, Italy. Caretti selects the best wood grains from smaller pieces of wood that he has cut to carve out the back, front, and neck of guitars.

tin can. In sum, the complexity of music depends less on technology than on human imagination.

The first step in the building of any instrument is the selection and preparation of material. Wood used for wind or stringed instruments needs to be seasoned, as do the reeds used in oboes, clarinets, saxophones, and related instruments. Metals, which are widely used for strings, bells, cymbals, gongs, trumpets, and horns, must be manufactured and cast—often originally by secret processes. Next, the construction and tuning of all instruments require skill and craftsmanship: the piercing of a tube to a uniform or expanding width, the flaring of the bell of a wind instrument to increase sonority, the measurement of the bars of a *saron* (for the Javanese gamelan) or of a glockenspiel, the curvature of the back of a lute or oud, the internal and external structure of the body of a violin, a koto, or even a *shakuhachi*. All of these involve accurate workmanship from experts in wood and metal and, in many instances, a knowledge of the mathematics of sound.

The mathematical basis of accurate tuning systems has been the subject of philosophical and scientific speculation since ancient times; nevertheless, no single system has been deemed perfect. All practical tuning systems involve a series of compromises, a fact that instrument makers have known for centuries.

The instrument maker's skill, like that of the cabinetmaker and the silversmith, was developed by long practice, and the principles that determine both tone and intonation were discovered by trial and error. The growth of instrumental playing in 16th-century Europe stimulated the production of instruments to be used not merely for ceremonial and official entertainment but also for social occasions and private pleasure. From this time, records began to be kept of the names of makers, many of whom established family businesses that lasted for several generations. These include, for example, Andrea Amati (16th century), a violin maker in Cremona, Italy; Hans Ruckers (late 16th century), a harpsichord maker in Antwerp, Belgium; and Johann Haas (1649–1723), a trumpet maker in Nürnberg (now in Germany). In all literate cultures there are known families or guilds of instrument makers, e.g., for the Middle Eastern oud, South Asian sitar and *vina*, or Japanese *tsuzumi* drums. Around the world, instrument makers have long signed their products. Although similar respectful positions are held by instrument makers in cultures without a written record, their reputation is far less likely to spread beyond their particular time and place.

Instrument makers have always represented a blend of conservatism with the ability to quickly seize on and use a new constructional technique, a new tool, or a new material. Their contribution to both the history of music and the history of musical instruments has been enormous and little appreciated. The older makers of instruments were craftsmen who took delight in the appearance of their work. In some cases, additions are purely decorative, as when pictures were painted on the inside of harpsichord lids or elaborate patterns were carved onto Indian *vinas* or inlaid into Persian lutes and drums. The rare set of 9th-century court instruments found in Nara, Japan, includes stunning examples of such artisan skills from all over East Asia. Equal beauty is found on many of the anonymously constructed instruments of Oceania. Often these additions are symbolic or totemic; the patterns on the Australian didjeridu identify the clan of the performer, and shapes and patterns on instruments in New Guinea reflect aspects of the environment and culture. Similarly, the dragon heads on the end of Tibetan and Chinese woodwinds have a symbolic meaning in those cultures. Most modern Western instruments reject ornamentation, but overall design and finish are as important as they have always been.

Modern technology has in many cases simplified or improved the construction of instruments. In the past, for example, the tubes of horns and trumpets were made from a sheet of brass cut to the right width, which was rolled into shape, leaving the edges to be joined by brazing. In modern manufacture the tube is drawn in one piece, and there is no seam. Evolution of design has been particularly notable in the construction of woodwind instruments, not only in the fixing of the metal keys and the mechanism that controls them but also in the piercing of holes in such a way that they are acoustically correct. This achievement was due mainly to the pioneering work of Theobald Boehm, who was not only a flute maker but also a performer and composer. His system, designed for the flute, was later applied to the clarinet, the oboe, and the bassoon. The early 19th century saw a revolution in the manufacture of brass instruments as well: the addition of pieces of tubing of different lengths through which the air could be directed by the depression of valves (or pistons), enabling an instrument to produce all 12 notes of the chromatic scale, in place of its earlier limitation to the notes of the natural harmonic (overtone) series. Newer techniques of cutting and beating metal have created distinctive modern instruments, such as steel drums.

The discovery of plastics in the 20th century also has influenced the manufacturers of instruments; for example, some makers have used plastic instead of quill or leather for the plectra that pluck the strings of the harpsichord, and plastic recorders have been built. Mechanization has made possible the mass production of instruments of all kinds. Insofar as this makes it possible for people to acquire an instrument at a moderate price, mass production is a good thing, and in education it has been beneficial to schools working on a small budget. A natural development has been the provision of kits consisting of the separate parts of an instrument, which can then be assembled by the purchaser. It remains true, however, that the production of an instrument of the finest quality still demands the highest degree of individual skill. A violin glued together from mass-produced parts cannot be the equal of one that has been meticulously constructed from the first by

A heckelphone is a double-reed woodwind instrument that resembles the baritone oboe.

an individual craftsman who will not be satisfied with his work until every detail of it has been tested.

Technology has been of service to music by providing composers with instruments they have asked for, by eliminating some defects of instruments, and by making instruments more widely available to the community in general. Richard Wagner, for example, suggested the need for a baritone double-reed instrument akin to the oboe; the resulting heckelphone has been featured in Richard Strauss's opera *Salome* (1905) and subsequent works. Wagner also ordered a special type of tuba for use in his four-opera cycle *Der Ring des Nibelungen* (*The Ring of the Nibelung*, 1869–76). Not all modern changes in construction have been wholly advantageous, however. It is easier to play in tune on a modern woodwind instrument, but the older examples, being less cluttered with metal fittings, had a purer tone. Similarly, the modern horn is to most listeners inferior in tone quality to its 18th-century predecessor. Among Western orchestral instruments, only the trombone and the stringed instruments have remained, apart from minor modifications, unchanged in structure over the centuries (though the substitution of wire strings for gut has materially altered the tone of the violin). In contrast, the rate of technological change in electronic instruments has been almost bewilderingly fast.

CLASSIFICATION OF INSTRUMENTS

Instruments have been classified in various ways, some of which overlap. The Chinese divide them according to the material of which they are made—as, for example, stone, wood, silk, and metal. Writers in the Greco-Roman world distinguished three main types of instruments: wind, stringed, and percussion. This classification was retained in the Middle Ages and persisted for several centuries: it is the one preferred by some writers, with the addition of electronic instruments, at the present day. Some 16th-century writers excluded certain instruments from this classification; the musical theorist Lodovico Zacconi went so far as to exclude all percussion instruments and established a fourfold division of his own—wind, keyed, bowed, and plucked.

A different fourfold classification was accepted by Hindus at least as early as the 1st century BCE: they recognized stringed instruments, wind instruments, percussion instruments of wood or metal, and percussion instruments with skin heads (i.e., drums). This ancient system—based on the material producing sound—was adopted by the Belgian instrument maker and acoustician Victor-Charles Mahillon, who named his four main classes autophones, or instruments made of a sonorous material that vibrates to produce sound (e.g., bells, rattles); membranophones, in which a stretched skin is caused to vibrate (e.g., drums); aerophones, in which the sound is produced by a vibrating column of air (wind instruments); and chordophones, or stringed instruments. In their highly influential studies of musical instruments, the Austrian musicologist Erich von Hornbostel and his German colleague Curt Sachs accepted and expanded Mahillon's basic division, creating the classification now used in most systematic studies of instruments. The name idiophones was substituted for autophones, and each class was subdivided according to a method similar to that used by botanists. A fifth class, electrophones, in which vibration is produced by oscillating electric circuits, was added later. The Table gives examples of instruments that fall within the various categories.

Classification and Examples of Some Musical Instruments

IDIOPHONES	
Struck against each other	cymbals, castanets
Struck with a beater	triangle, glockenspiel, xylophone, slit drums
Shaken	rattle, jingles
Scraped	scraper
Plucked	jew's harp, music box
Rubbed	musical glasses
MEMBRANOPHONES	
Struck	side drum, bass drum, timpani
Rubbed	friction drum
Blown	mirliton (or kazoo)
CHORDOPHONES	
Zithers	
Plucked	harpsichord
Struck	hammered dulcimer, piano
Lutes	
Plucked	lute, guitar
Bowed	violin, viola da gamba
Lyres	
Plucked	Greek *kithara*, Ethiopian *beganna*
Bowed	Welsh *crwth*
Harp	Celtic small harp, orchestral chromatic harp

(*CONTINUED ON THE NEXT PAGE*)

(CONTINUED FROM THE PREVIOUS PAGE)

AEROPHONES	
Free (air not confined)	
Without keyboard	bull-roarer, harmonica
With keyboard	harmonium, melodeon
Flutes (air blown against an edge)	recorder, flute
Reedpipes	
Single reed	clarinet, saxophone
Double reed	shawm, crumhorn, oboe, bassoon, sarrusophone
Lipped (air blown through player's vibrating lips)	horn, cornet, trumpet, trombone, tuba, serpent
ELECTROPHONES	
Monophonic (producing a single line of melody)	theremin, trautonium, ondes martenot
Polyphonic (producing harmony and simultaneous melodic lines)	many synthesizers

Many instruments can be played using more than one system of tone production and hence might reasonably appear in several subcategories. The double bass, for example, is usually considered a chordophone whose strings may be bowed or plucked; sometimes, however, the body of the instrument is slapped or struck, placing the double bass among the idiophones. The tambourine is a membranophone insofar as it has a skin head which is struck; but, if it is only shaken so that its jingles sound, it should be classed as an idiophone, for in this operation the skin head is irrelevant. Open flue stops are the foundation of organ tone, but the instrument also has a number of free reed stops, so that the organ belongs equally to the first and second order of aerophones. Modern composers not infrequently require players to treat their instruments in unorthodox ways, thus changing their position in the classification system.

It must be understood that the Sachs-Hornbostel system was created for the purpose of bringing order to the massive collections of musical instruments in ethnographic museums. It is directly analogous to the various book classification systems of libraries and, like them, is arbitrary. Musicians themselves generally think of instruments in terms of their technological features and playing method. To them, therefore, it is logical to group keyboard instruments together, ignoring the fact that in the Sachs-Hornbostel system such instruments fit into several categories.

HISTORY AND EVOLUTION

There has been speculation about the origin of instruments since antiquity. Older writers were generally content to rely on mythology or legends. In the 19th century, partly as a result of theories of evolution put forward by Charles Darwin and Herbert Spencer, new chronologies based on anthropological evidence were advanced. The British writer John Frederick Rowbotham argued that there was originally a drum stage, followed by a pipe stage, and finally a lyre stage. The Austrian writer Richard Wallaschek, on the other hand, maintained that, although rhythm was the primal element, the pipe came first, followed by song, and the drum last. Sachs based his chronology on archaeological excavation and the geographic distribution of the instruments found in them. Following this method, he established three main strata. The first stratum, which is found all over the world, consists of simple idiophones and aerophones; the second stratum, less widely distributed, adds drums and simple stringed instruments; the third, occurring only in certain areas, adds xylophones, drum-sticks, and more complex flutes. In the 21st century, ethnomusicologists have questioned assumptions about the evolution of instruments from simple to complex.

The development of musical instruments among ancient high civilizations in Asia, North Africa, and the Mediterranean appears to have emphasized stringed instruments. In Central and South America, wind and struck instruments seem to have been most important. It is not always easy to say whether instruments are indig-enous to a particular area, however, since their cultivation may well have spread from one country to another through trade or migration. Nevertheless, it is known that the harp was used from early times in Mesopotamia, Egypt, and India and was imported into China after the end of the 4th century CE. In Greece it was regarded as a foreign instrument: the standard plucked instru-ment was the lyre, known in its fully developed form as the *kithara* (or *cithara*). Apart from the trumpet, the only wind instrument in normal use in Greece was the *aulos*, a double-reed instrument akin to the modern oboe. The Egyptians used wind instruments not only with double reeds but also with single reeds and thus may be said to have anticipated the clarinet. Peculiar to China was the *sheng*, or mouth organ; the Chinese also used as an artistic instrument the panpipes (*xiao*), which in Greece had a recreational function.

In medieval Europe, many instruments came from Asia, having been transmitted through Byzantium, Spain, or eastern Europe. Perhaps the most notable development in western Europe was the practice, originating apparently in the 15th century, of building instruments in families, from the smallest to the largest size. A typical family was that of the shawms, which were powerful double-reed instruments. A distinction was made between *haut* (loud) and *bas* (soft) instruments, the former being suitable for performance out-of-doors and the latter for more intimate occasions. Hence, the shawm came to be known as the hautbois (loud wood), and this name was transferred to its more delicately toned descendant, the 17th-century oboe. By the beginning of the 17th century the German musical writer and composer Michael Praetorius, in his *Syntagma musicum* ("Musical Treatise"), was able to give a detailed account of families of instruments of all kinds—recorders, flutes, shawms, trombones, viols, and violins.

PERCUSSION INSTRUMENTS

Drum ensembles have achieved extraordinary sophistication in Africa, and the small hand-beaten drum is of great musical significance in western Asia and India. The native cultures of the Americas have always made extensive use of drums, as well as other struck and shaken instruments. In Southeast Asia and parts of Africa, xylophones and, since the introduction of metals, their cousins the metallophones play significant roles. Europe, however, has not placed great emphasis on drums and other percussion instruments.

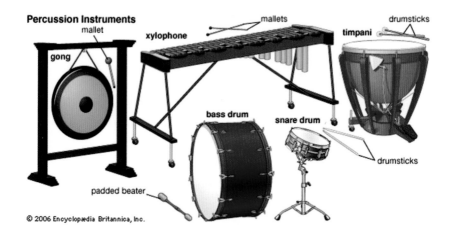

Percussion Instruments

mallet

gong

xylophone

mallets

timpani

drumsticks

bass drum

snare drum

drumsticks

padded beater

© 2006 Encyclopædia Britannica, Inc.

Some of the percussion instruments of the Western orchestra include (*counterclockwise, from top*) xylophone, gong, bass drum, snare drum, and timpani.

STRINGED INSTRUMENTS

Many varieties of plucked instruments were found in Europe during the Middle Ages and the Renaissance; but bowed instruments eventually came to characterize the area, and they played an important role in the rest of Eurasia and in North Africa as well. The idea of playing a stringed instrument with a bow may have originated with the horse cultures of Central Asia, perhaps in the 9th century CE. The technique then spread rapidly over most of the European landmass.

The European fiddle existed in various forms: by the 16th century these had settled down into two distinct types—the viol, known in Italy as viola da gamba (leg

A viola, side and front views, is seen here. A stringed instrument, the viola is the tenor of the violin family.

fiddle), and the violin, or *viola da braccio* (arm fiddle). The viol has a flat back, sloping shoulders, and six or seven strings; the violin has a rounded back, rounded shoulders, and four strings. The viol, unlike the violin, has frets—pieces of gut wound at intervals around the fingerboard—which make every stopped note (i.e., the string being pressed by the finger to produce a higher pitch) sound like an open (unstopped) string. The violin, being the smallest member of the family, came to be known by the diminutive *violino*: the tenor of the family was called simply viola, while the bass acquired the name violoncello, a diminutive of *violone* ("big fiddle").

KEYBOARD INSTRUMENTS

Only in Europe did the keyboard develop—for reasons that are not clear. The principle of the keyboard has been used successfully to control bells (the carillon), plucked and struck stringed instruments (the piano and harpsichord), and wind instruments (the organ, the accordion, and the harmonium).

Of all instruments, the organ showed the most remarkable development from the early Middle Ages to the 17th century. Originally, sound was admitted to the pipes by withdrawing sliders or depressing levers. Both of these methods were clumsy: they gave way to a reduction in the size of the levers, which eventually could be depressed by the fingers, while the larger pipes were controlled by pedals. A further development was to separate the various rows of pipes, so that each row could be brought into action or suppressed by means of a draw stop. Once a manageable keyboard had been produced, it could be applied to the portable organ, carried by the player, which was already in use by the 12th century. Scientific experiments with the monochord, a stretched string that could be divided into various lengths by means of a metal tangent, were followed by the construction of an instrument with a whole range of strings and a keyboard similar to that of the organ—the clavichord. A similar adaptation of the plucking of stringed instruments led to the harpsichord, the ingenious mechanism of which had been perfected by the 16th century. It is curious that a similar method was not applied to the dulcimer, which was struck with hammers, until the early 18th century, when the Italian maker

Bartolomeo Cristofori constructed the first pianoforte, so-called because, unlike the harpsichord, it could vary the tone from soft (piano) to loud (forte).

WIND INSTRUMENTS

In Europe the practice of constructing instruments in families continued from the 17th century onward. English composers wrote for the tenor hautbois, the intermediate oboe d'amore, and the bass, or baritone, oboe. The clarinet (the name means "little trumpet") emerged at the end of the 17th century and, like the oboe, developed into a family extending to a contrabass clarinet in the 19th century and later a subcontrabass. It established itself only gradually in the orchestra in the course of the 18th century.

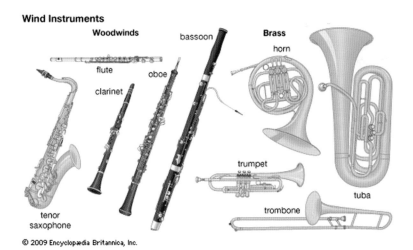

Wind Instruments

Woodwinds — flute, clarinet, oboe, bassoon, tenor saxophone

Brass — horn, trumpet, trombone, tuba

© 2009 Encyclopædia Britannica, Inc.

Some of the wind instruments of the Western orchestra include (*left to right, top to bottom*) tenor saxophone, flute, clarinet, oboe, bassoon, trumpet, horn, trombone, and tuba.

Trumpets and horns were used in most areas of Eurasia for ceremonial and military purposes. They remained relatively unchanged until the early 19th century, when valves were added to European instruments. This modification also led to the creation of new types. A pioneer in the field was the Belgian instrument maker Antoine-Joseph Sax, who in 1845 built a family of valved instruments called saxhorns, using the bugle as the basis for his invention. Similar instruments were widely adopted in military and brass bands, but only the bass, under the name bass tuba, became a normal member of the orchestra. Sax also invented the saxophone, a single-reed instrument like the clarinet but with a conical tube. This, too, was made in various sizes, which came to be used both in military bands and in jazz ensembles. The saxophone never became a normal member of the symphony orchestra, but the alto and the tenor have been used

ADOLPHE SAX

Antoine-Joseph "Adolphe" Sax (1814–1894) was a Belgian-French maker of musical instruments and inventor of the saxophone.

Sax was the son of Charles Joseph Sax (1791–1865), a maker of wind and brass instruments, as well as of pianos, harps, and guitars. Adolphe studied the flute and clarinet at the Brussels Conservatory and in 1842 went to Paris. There he exhibited the saxophone, a single-reed instrument made of metal, with a conical bore, overblowing at the octave, which had resulted from his efforts to improve the tone of the bass clarinet. It was patented in 1846. With his father he evolved the saxhorn (patented 1845), a development on the bugle horn; the saxo-tromba, producing a tone between that of the bugle and the trumpet; and the saxtuba. Sax discovered that it is the proportions given to a column of air vibrating in a sonorous tube, and these alone, that determine the timbre produced.

In 1857 Sax was appointed instructor of the saxophone at the Paris Conservatory. Later he improved several instruments and invented others without, however, establishing a basis for their commercial exploitation. Many of his instruments were accepted for the French army bands, and for 10 years Sax was involved in lawsuits with competing instrument makers seeking to have his patents revoked. In his 80th year he was living in abject poverty; Emmanuel Chabrier, Jules Massenet, and Camille Saint-Saëns were obliged to petition the minister of fine arts to come to his aid.

by art-music composers, largely as solo instruments, and occasionally a complete quartet of four different sizes has appeared in an orchestral work.

ENSEMBLES

The variety of musical ensembles used throughout the world is vast and beyond description, but the following principles apply nearly everywhere. Outdoor music, which is often ceremonial, most frequently involves the use of loud wind instruments and drums. Indoor music, which is more often intended for passive listening, emphasizes such quieter instruments as bowed and plucked strings and flutes.

The establishment of orchestras, as opposed to chamber groups, in the early 17th century led to a slight revision of these principles in Europe. The orchestra's sound is founded on a large ensemble of bowed strings, but it adds the previously outdoor instruments (wind and percussion) for colour and climax. As concert halls increased in size and popularity, so too did the sound-volume requirements of so-called indoor instruments. One result was that the violin family was favoured at the expense of the quieter viols. The latter, along with other instruments whose tone was too weak for orchestral music, gradually dropped out of use until the 20th century, when earlier styles of music and their associated instruments experienced a revival in popularity.

AUTOMATIC INSTRUMENTS

Water power, clockwork, steam, and electricity have all been used at various times to power musical instruments, enabling them to produce sound automatically. Examples include church bells, automatic organs, musical clocks, automatic pianos and harpsichords, music boxes, calliopes, and even automatic orchestras. Most of the impetus behind this phenomenon ceased with the development of the phonograph and other recording devices of the 20th century.

ELECTRIC AND ELECTRONIC INSTRUMENTS

The development of electricity led not only to its use for mechanical purposes—for example, to control the key action and wind flow in the organ—but also as a means of amplification (e.g., in the vibraphone). With advances in electronics technology, players can now also make use of computers to generate and store tones and musical patterns. The growth of companies manufacturing electronic and digital instruments has been rapid, and the use of electronic equipment, such as sound synthesizers and recorders using analog or digital media, to produce and combine sound unrelated to the musical scale has become common.

Modern electronic instruments and equipment include light-emitting audiocubes. Audiocubes in effect can "shape sound." This technology has been adapted as an aid in composition as well as live performance.

Another invention is the Reactable. It was developed in the early 2000s by a music technology team at a Spanish university whose objective was to develop "the best computer-based musical instrument we could imagine." The Reactable operates on a backlit tabletop on which are placed electronic

Band members play an electric bass guitar (*left*), an electronic keyboard or synthesizer (*background*), drums (*right*), and a synthesizer (*foreground, right*). A controller and mixer board are seen in the foreground.

blocks called tangibles, which combine to function as a type of synthesizer. Several people can collaborate. Commercial sales of Reactables began in 2009, and they have been used by rock bands in live performance.

MUSICAL PERFORMANCE AND EXPRESSION

The performance setting and the way perform-ers express a musical work complete the music experience from composer to listener. Performers' choices of instrumentation, arrangement, inter-pretation, and delivery profoundly impact how the composition will be received.

Musical performance is the step in the musical process during which musical ideas are realized and transmitted to a listener. In Western music, perfor-mance is most commonly viewed as an interpretive art, though it is not always merely that. Performers to some degree determine aspects of any music they play. Issues of tempo, phrasing, dynamics, and, in some types of music, pitches and instrumentation are sub-ject to a performer's discretion.

Musical expression is that element of musical performance that is something more than mere notes. Western music is notated on a system that specifies pitch and the relative lengths of notes. Factors such as speed or dynamics are usually indicated only by words or abbreviations. Similarly, directions to the performer regarding technique, often with particular musical consequences, are mostly expressible by words. But the finer musical points are more difficult to indicate and must eventually stem from the performer himself or from a performance tradition with which he is familiar. This chapter considers musical performance and expression.

PERFORMANCE

Because the pleasure people derive from sounds has always been closely related to the pleasure they derive from making the sounds themselves, it is difficult to conceive of the origin of music as separate from an act of musical performance. Models for the establishment of rhythm may be found in heartbeat and breathing, and in the inflections of speech and cries of grief, pleasure, and desire are found the source of what became song.

The earliest visual manifestations of musical performance are found in rock paintings and excavated objects. While the interrelationship of music and ritual is clear, there is evidence that music was performed for dancing, in various work activities, and games as well. Flutelike instruments of many sizes, made from bones and wood, and elaborate percussion instruments figure prominently in all early cultures, in which these instruments often were assigned symbolic significance associated with forces of the supernatural.

Singing is most probably the oldest musical activity. Even in the most archaic cultures the singer had a special, defined position. In early singing there are three classes of sound: the first is called logogenic, in which words form the basis for the wavering musical incantation; the second, called pathogenic, consists of harsh, forceful, percussive, nonverbal sounds emitted to express strong feeling; in the third category, called melogenic, the sounds of the two previous categories combine to form a contour of pitches that pursue a course seemingly dictated by the weight of tensions inherent in the sequence of pitches and hence melodic in effect.

Early societies evolved several means to relieve the monotony of one person's singing. A principle device is called antiphony, which involved two groups that sang in alternation or a leader who sang and was answered by a group of singers. In the latter may be seen the origin of responsorial singing, which continues today and which may be the point of origin for several types of musical phrase structures. Polyphony was also antici-pated in early musical performance. It appeared through haphazard rather than intentional manifestations, such as the singing of the same melody with the parts start-ing on different pitches or at different times.

ASPECTS OF WESTERN MUSICAL PERFORMANCE

Music as an interpretive art is a relatively recent phenomenon. In ancient societies, music plays a ritual role based on an oral tradition, and each performer in a sense interprets the tradition but, more impor-tantly, renews it and transforms it through personal performance.

THE PERFORMER AS INTERPRETER

The development of the performer's role as interpreter coincided with the development of musical notation.

Because composers for so many centuries were in a position to supervise the performances of their music, certain aspects of performance were not notated. Notation has grown increasingly complex as the dissemination of printed music has become more widespread. Ultimately, the degree of judgment a performer may exercise is determined by the period in which the music was composed. For music of certain periods, even though their notational systems are incomplete and give few indications of how the music should sound beyond pitch and rhythm, musical scholarship has amassed much information concerning proper instrumentation, ornamentation, improvisation, and other traditional performing practices that determine to a large degree the sound and stylistic character of the music. Performers as interpreters operate within a range of limitations imposed upon them by their understanding of the printed page, whatever knowledge may be available concerning the tradition that surrounds the music at hand, and the extent to which their personal tastes coincide with this information. Certain aspects of the musical taste of the past sometimes cease to be expressive and gradually disappear from usage. Just as often, with the passage of time, performers tend to reassess the literature of previous ages and find renewed interest in practices that an earlier generation may have set aside. In any case, performers as interpreters speak to and with the tastes of their own time. And their task, no different from that of the earliest performers, is to renew, to refine, and to enrich the materials and traditions they inherit.

MEDIUMS OF PERFORMANCE

The mediums for musical performance are extraordinarily various. Western technology has had a tremendous impact on the development of musical instruments and has thereby greatly expanded the means whereby music is made. Performance may be vocal, instrumental, or electronic. Vocal performance is the oldest and the primary influence for the development of all subsequent musical gestures and materials. Instrumental music began with the development of percussion instruments and crude horns; stringed instruments came later. Electronic music was a 20th-century development involving the reproduction of traditional performance mediums through electronic means, while it also evolved composition and performance of its own. At first it reproduced natural sounds by electronic means; later, composers and technicians began to invent electronic sounds and to discover new sound relationships.

In all musical mediums the solo performance is the most spectacular. The power of music to compel attention and to stir emotions lends to the solo performer an especially fascinating aura. This is the domain of the virtuoso, that musical performing phenomenon of prodigious technical mastery, invention, and charisma. Most solo literature includes another instrument or group of instruments, and the literature varies from one medium to another according to the expressive range and technical capabilities of the solo instrument.

The largest solo literature for a single instrument is for keyboard instruments. Vocal solo literature is very important and extensive, and the stringed instruments also have a distinguished solo repertoire. The wind, brass, and percussion solo literature is more restricted.

In vocal and instrumental chamber ensemble performance, the performing groups are divided into duets, trios, quartets, quintets, sextets, septets, and octets, which exist for every medium and combination. Of particular importance is a string quartet consisting of two violins, viola, and cello. Dating from the 18th century, this instrumental ensemble is analogous to the vocal ensemble consisting of soprano, alto, tenor, and bass.

Symphonic music dates from the 17th century. With the rise of the middle class and its aspirations for culture, music as an art required performing situations that would accommodate more people. Larger halls required ensembles acoustically suited to the expanded performing areas. The primary result of this development was the symphony orchestra with

The Los Angeles Philharmonic, led by conductor Gustavo Dudamel, performs in Walt Disney Concert Hall at the opening night gala in 2015. The Frank Gehry–designed hall is celebrated for its state-of-the-art acoustics.

its multiple stringed, wind, brass, and percussion instruments.

Ensemble performance places a special responsibility on the concentration of the individual performers, who must attend not only to their own playing but also to that of all the others in the ensemble. All aspects of the performance depend on this mutual awareness. The leader of most small ensembles is one of the performers, the first violinist, a keyboard player, or one of the singers who indicates tempi, entrances, and musical character and supervises rehearsals. As ensembles grew in size and complexity and their problems of coordination increased, the leader set aside performance on an instrument and focused on the beating of time and the communication through clear hand signals of the appropriate moment for entrances, tempo changes, dynamic accents, and the shaping of phrases. This leader is called a conductor. The role of the conductor often is analogous to that of a soloist in the attention of an audience, though the conductor makes no musical sound. As they are chiefly responsible for the music orchestras play, both in terms of choice and execution, conductors have had considerable impact on the development of music.

Opera, the marriage of music and drama, is the most complex performance situation. It entails much more than a single performer or group of performers, their instruments, and a hall in which to play. Text, decor, costumes, histrionic projection, preparation time, as well as singers, instrumentalists, and a bevy of extramusical technicians, must all be brought together and coordinated into the final production.

ARTISTIC TEMPERAMENT

Many forces interact in developing those traits that distinguish various performing traditions and individual performers. Personality and temperament fundamentally affect the manner in which a performer works, as does the cultural milieu. There are performers who use music as a vehicle for display and others for whom performance is only a means to illuminate the music. Nor does performance necessarily mean public performance. For some people musical performance is essentially private, requiring no confirmation in the form of audience approval. The musical pleasure of such people rests solely on performing, either alone or with other musicians. Much chamber music is played under these private circumstances, and much music has been written for such situations. This used to be the primary realm of the musical amateur, a skilled but nonprofessional music lover whose ranks are ever diminishing.

The type of performing situation at the opposite end of the spectrum is one directed to securing audience attention and affection. The need for audience approval has led to innovations as well as some decadence in its impact on the musical scene: innovation, if the performer is led to discover imaginative and fresh means of attracting public acclaim; decadence, if the devices for audience attraction become cheap and thinly spectacular, when the performer may distract the audience from more deserving work and debase its taste.

Intuition and intellect figure prominently in the temperament of a musical performer. Intuition is the capacity to do the musically "right" thing without instruction or special consideration of the alternatives. Intellect is the means whereby musicians enlarge the range of their instincts through the pursuit of new information, reflection, and analysis of the musical material at hand. Each element informs and completes the other.

Many musicians depend heavily on intuition in solving performance problems. Their solutions are often imaginative and fresh and their performances exciting. Others pursue a methodical path as they examine minutely relevant musical details. They analyze thoroughly the scores they perform, comparing manuscript facsimiles and various printed editions, and attempt to discover new musical relationships, new ways of delineating these relationships in performance, and, in short, new ideas as to how the music might best be played and how it should sound. Art, poetry, biography, cultural history, and any material relating to the period of the piece of music being studied for performance may be sources of musical insight for the performer.

NATIONAL CHARACTERISTICS

At various times in history, national origin has been considered an important delineating characteristic in musical performance. This is partly the result of certain consistent emphases and features in the music written by composers of different nationalities. The Italians' interest in the voice has evolved bel canto, a special quality derived from vocal music, which has carried over into their music for instruments (the stringed instruments especially), and into the general texture of Italian music, which has always given melody special prominence.

The English have had a highly developed and sophisticated musical performance tradition. Amateur improvisation figured importantly in its early history. While this has perhaps tended toward a conservative musical atmosphere, it has also produced a high standard for performance. The French have maintained a strong sense of national identity in their performing arts. In music their concerns for orderly design, delicate expressiveness, simplicity, naturalness, and beauty of sound extend back for centuries. Articulate philosophical and structural considerations have played important roles in developing nationalistic traits in the German tradition of musical performance.

The rich folklorist traditions of Spain, Hungary, and Russia have influenced rhythm, melody, and sonority in Western musical performing traditions. The Russian schools of string and piano technique have greatly advanced the performance resources of these instruments in the past 100 years. The United States, younger and more heterogeneous, has had a shorter musical history but an abundance of great symphony orchestras and solo artists, who are in demand because of their precise execution, versatility, and breadth of repertoire.

HISTORICAL STYLISTIC DEVELOPMENTS

In antiquity the Sumerians, Egyptians, Greeks, and Romans evolved the first aesthetic theories and musical systems relevant to the music of the modern Western world. Unfortunately, few actual musical examples survive because of early notational practices and the gradual erosion of oral traditions. What is known is derived from the writings of the period and iconography—depictions of performing musicians, instruments, and musical events in sculpture and in wall and vase paintings.

In this miniature from the Codex Manesse, c. 1300, Otto IV of Brandenburg is depicted playing chess with a lady while jongleurs and troubadours perform for them.

In the Middle Ages traditions of musical performance were kept alive by the church and in the music sung and played by wandering minstrels.

In the Renaissance, polyphony (combining several simultaneous voice parts) and the early precursors of modern tonality (organization of music around a focal tone) were developed. The smooth flow of Renaissance liturgical counterpoint (polyphony) and the perky rhythms of secular Renaissance dance music remained as models of taste and musical technique even into the 21st century.

The performer emerged as a central figure in the focus of musical attention and purpose during the Baroque period. The heightening of the role of the individual performing artist and the invention of increasingly dramatic gestures to demonstrate performers' skills combined with a steady refinement in the construction of musical instruments. The reduction of musical materials to two modes (scale and melody patterns), in this case the major and minor scales, and the initial efforts to compose with large musical forms (opera, oratorio, sonata, and concerto) took place in this period. It is notable that in the Baroque era the equal-temperament system for tuning the strings or pipes of keyboard instruments evolved—a development that has had a profound effect on the nature of musical language.

In the Rococo or Classical period that followed, the elaborate contrapuntal texture of Baroque music gave way to music of subtle dynamic differentiation, often based on simple folk materials (rhythms and melodies). The relationships between tonal materials and large musical forms achieved their highest state in the sonata and in opera.

The Romantic age was a period of refinement and intensification of Rococo principles with heavy literary overtones. It was the true age of the star virtuoso; that is, the age in which the role, person, and effect of the virtuoso was most dramatized and glamourized. The symphony orchestra in this period achieved its maximum development. Italian opera under Giuseppe Verdi found its noblest expression and German opera with Richard Wagner expanded into the *Gesamtkunstwerk* ("complete art work").

Modern music dates from an era beginning roughly around World War I. Concert life, however, has remained more or less what the 19th century established; the virtuoso conductor and performer dominate the musical establishment. By contrast, an ever-broadening spectrum of performance techniques and styles has been employed by small combos—jazz, rock, improvisational, experimental, live electronic, and multimedia—that have sprung up since the mid-20th century.

THE DEVELOPMENT OF WESTERN MUSICAL PERFORMANCE

Western traditions of musical performance have evolved throughout history. The music of early civilizations—those of Sumer and Egypt, for example—had much in common. Music was an important component of religion, and early stringed, wind, and percussive instruments were very much alike from culture to culture.

The way people experience modern electronic and digital music seems quite different. There remain, however, underlying similarities, and connections with the past can be traced.

ANTIQUITY

The civilizations of antiquity expanded the role assigned to music in earlier cultures. The Sumerians established the foundations for the tradition of liturgical music. Some of the prayers that they sang have survived. From various artifacts of this civilization something is known about Sumerian musical instruments and some of the situations in which music was played. Such instruments as lyres, harps, sistra, pipes, timbrels, and various drums figured importantly. Particular instruments were identified as accompaniment with specific types of religious poetry, and indeed the development of different poetic genres seems to have been considerably influenced by the nature of these instruments. While its primary purpose was religious, music also had something of a secular role in Sumerian culture and was played in processions, at banquets, and during sporting events. Music as a profession first developed in Sumerian culture. Both men and women participated as singers and instrumentalists and held priestlike positions with specific functions and ranks of authority.

The musical culture of ancient Egypt, which apparently emerged from the same sources as Sumer, resembles that earlier culture in many aspects: the close relationship between music and religion, the presence of a musical profession, some secular musical activity, and similar musical instruments. Of special interest in Egyptian music is the development of chironomy, the use of hand signals to indicate to instrumentalists what they should play. The singer in this manner guided instrumentalists through melodies with which the singer was seemingly more familiar than the players.

In these ancient cultures there was no notational system or codified theory of musical practice. Different musical traditions were exchanged in the process of trade, migration, military conquest, and intermarriage to form that common body of practices that is the basis of Western music.

Of the early civilizations, Greece provided the musical culture of greatest significance for the development of Western music. The system of scales and modes, as well as a large part of the general philosophy concerning the nature and effect of musical sounds, has been inherited from the Greeks. It was also the Greeks who developed the theory of ethos, which defines the character of psychological and emotional response to different musical stimuli. Building on the ancient religions and magical accoutrements of music, the Greeks assigned specific mental and emotional states to specific pitch arrangements and instrumental combinations. Music infused with this motivating power stood at the centre of the social order.

Though a major part of Western musical terminology, basic music theory and philosophy, basic notational practices, and the foundations of acoustical physics derive from the ancient Greeks, very little of their music has survived. The great ethical significance of music in Greek society caused performing mastery to be an essential aspect of education. Everyone was taught to sing and to play instruments. For a major part of the period all music was a setting of words with instrumental accompaniment, for the most part doubling the voice at the interval of octaves, fourths, or fifths. It was only in the later part of the period, after the age of Pericles (late 5th century BCE), that instruments began to be played independently of singers.

Music, in the later stages of the Hellenic period, became an increasingly important part of public spectacles. As musical performance became increasingly secularized and became the property of the masses, the upper classes withdrew to esoteric considerations of the art and reflections on its past. It was perhaps at this point that music was divided into two fairly artificial categories: the contemplation of music's nature and history and practical musical performance.

Assuming the artistic mantle of ancient Greece, the Romans disseminated Greek music throughout the known world. The essential role of music in the Roman Empire remained unchanged. Rome's principal contribution consisted in serving as a catalyst for the mixing of Hebraic and Hellenic traditions of musical performance, which, preserved by the Christian Church for a thousand years, emerged again in the Renaissance into the first flowering of modern musical practices in the West.

Although not in the mainstream of Western musical performance, Islamic (North African and Middle Eastern) classical music closely approaches the orchestral tradition of European music in one respect: large choruses and orchestras—consisting of tambourines, pot drums, recorder-flutes, ouds (plucked lutes), bowed lutes, and dulcimers—are assembled to perform "suites" consisting of a series of instrumental solos and orchestral selections interspersed with unison choral songs or solo recitatives based on classical poetry. But while these suites are perfectly suited to performance in formal concert halls, they may also be heard in much less regulated settings, such as cafés. Here the listener is free either to concentrate intellectually on the progress and development of the musical ideas or to converse and eat, relaxing in the beauty of the general musical design. The more "oriental" side of Islamic musical performance is more improvisatory, either in solo performance on a recorder-flute, fiddle, oud, or dulcimer or by any of these in combination with the voice—the instrumentalist then elaborating on the singer's improvisation. Here, too, the relationship of audience to performer is much less formal than in the performance of European music.

THE MIDDLE AGES

The tradition of sung prayers and psalms extends into the shadows of early civilization. Such sacred singing was often accompanied by instruments, and its rhythmic character was marked. In the synagogue, however, the sung prayers were often unaccompanied. Ritual dance was excluded from the synagogue as the rhythmic character of sacred music surrendered its more sensual aspects. Even in the prayers themselves, rhythmic verse gave way to prose. The exclusion of women, the elevation of unison singing, and the exclusion of instruments served to establish a clear differentiation between musical performance in the synagogue and that of the street.

The musical performance tradition of the Christian Church grew out of the liturgical tradition of Judaism. The melodic formulas for the singing of psalms and the sung recitation of other scriptural passages are clearly based on Hebraic models.

Music in the Roman Catholic liturgy was performed mainly for the mass. Originally, the music was performed by the priest and the congregation, until, in time, there emerged from the congregation a special group of singers, called the choir, who assumed the musical role of answering and contrasting the solo singing of the priest. Women participated actively in musical performances in the ancient Christian Church until 578, when older Hebraic practices excluding them were restored. From that time until the 20th century, Roman Catholic Church choirs were composed solely of men and boys.

The first codification of early church music was reputedly made by Pope Gregory I during his reign (590–604). Gregory's collection was selected from chants already in use. His codification assigned these chants to particular services in the liturgical calendar. In general it reinforced the simple, spiritual, aesthetic quality of liturgical music. The music in this collection serves as a model of melodic design even in the 21st century and is regarded as one of the monuments of Western musical literature. This school of unison liturgical singing is called plainchant, plainsong, or Gregorian chant. Specific details concerning the manner in which chant was performed have been lost. There are speculations that the quality of sound the singers employed was somewhat thinner and more nasal than that used by contemporary singers. The authentic rhythmic style of chant cannot be ascertained. There is a theory, however, that the basic rhythmic units had the same durational value and were grouped in irregularly alternating groups of twos and threes. Pitch levels and tempos apparently varied somewhat according to the occasion. There are preserved manuscript notations reminding singers to be careful and modest in their work, indicating that temptations of inattention and excessive vocal display existed for even the earliest liturgical musicians.

While modern musical traditions in the West are based to a large extent on the principles of antiquity preserved in the notated music of the early church, a secular musical practice did exist; but because of the pervasive influence of the church, the dividing line between sacred and secular aspects was thin throughout a good part of the medieval period.

Several types of later secular song have survived. The musical notations are for the most part inadequate to give an accurate impression of the music, but it is known that it retained the essential monophonic character of liturgical music. One curious type of secular song, conductus, originated in the church itself. This song did not use traditional liturgical melodies or texts but was composed to be sung in the liturgical dramas or for processions. For this reason it dealt occasionally with subjects not religious in character. The goliard songs dating from the 11th century are among the oldest examples of secular music. They were the often bawdy Latin songs of itinerant theological students who roamed rather disreputably from school to school in the period preceding the founding of the great university centres in the 13th century.

Several other groups of medieval performers developed literary and musical genres based on vernacular texts: the jongleurs, a group of traveling entertainers in western Europe who sang, did tricks, and danced to earn their living; the troubadours in the south of France and the trouvères in the north; and the minnesingers, a class of artist-knights who wrote and sang love songs tinged with religious fervour.

Instruments, such as the *vielle*, harp, psaltery, flute, shawm, bagpipe, and drums were all used during the Middle Ages to accompany dances and singing. Trumpets and horns were used by nobility, and organs, both portative (movable) and positive (stationary), appeared in the larger churches. In general, little is known of secular instrumental music before the 13th century. It is doubtful that it had a role of any importance apart from accompaniment. Yet the possibility of accompanied liturgical music has not been eliminated by modern scholars.

The medieval musical development with the furthest-reaching consequences for musical performance was that of polyphony, a development directly related, as indicated above, to the experience of performing liturgical chant. For performers and performance, perhaps the most important developments in the wake of polyphony were refinements of rhythmic notation necessary to keep independent melodic lines synchronous. At first the obvious visual method of vertical alignment was used; later, as upper voices became more elaborate in comparison with the (chant-derived) lower ones, and writing in score thus wasted space, more symbolic methods of notating rhythm developed, most importantly in and around the new cathedral of Notre-Dame in Paris.

In the 14th century, partly because of the declining political strength of the church, the setting for new developments in music shifted from the sacred field to the secular, from the church to the court. This shift led in turn to a new emphasis on instrumental music and performance. Already the lower voices began to be performed on instruments—both because their long notes made them difficult to sing and because their texts (of only a few syllables) became senseless outside their original liturgical positions. Now, as secular princes became increasingly important patrons of composers and performers—a situation that would continue well into the 18th century—secular and instrumental music flourished. The polyphonic music of the church merged with the poetic art of the troubadours, and the two most important composers of the age were the blind Florentine organist Francesco Landini and the French poet Guillaume de Machaut, canon of Reims.

Most of the music of these composers seems to have been intended for combined vocal-instrumental performance, although this is seldom expressly indicated in the manuscripts. Medieval composers probably had no rigid expectations about performance media. Until the 17th century, and even through the 19th in the case of domestic performance, choice of instruments was likely to be dependent as much on available performers as on anything else. Many sources do, however, indicate that medieval musicians tended to separate instruments into two groups, loud and soft (*haut* and *bas*, or, very generally, wind and string), and to prefer contrasting sonorities within those groups for maximum differentiation of the individual parts. Outdoor or ceremonial music would be performed with loud instruments (shawm, bombard, trombone, organ); room music, with soft ones (lute, viol, recorder, harp). Paintings and manuscript illuminations of the period show that much secular performance included both a wide variety of bells, drums, and other percussion instruments and instruments with drones—bagpipes, fiddles, double recorders, hurdy-gurdies. The parts for these instruments are never found in the musical sources and must be reconstructed for modern performance.

The notation of medieval music often is misleading for the modern performer. Accidentals (sharps and flats, called then musica ficta) were often omitted as being understood. Further, it seems likely that variation, embellishment, and improvisation were very important elements of medieval performance. It is known that sections of some 15th-century two-part vocal music were enhanced by an extempore third part, in a technique called fauxbourdon; the notation of the 15th-century *basse danse* consisted of only a single line of unmeasured long notes, evidently used by the performing group of three instrumentalists for improvisation, much as a modern jazz combo's chart.

THE RENAISSANCE

The very concept of improvisation as a mere subcategory within performance practice could arise only after the invention of music printing, which had at first little discernible effect on performance. Extemporized ornamentation of polyphonic music continued and increased during the 16th century in instrumental, vocal, and combined performance, both secular and sacred. Later in the century, liturgical music again became less extravagant in the wake of the Council of Trent (1545–63), which ordered that masses be sung "clearly and at the right speed" and that singing "be constituted not to give empty pleasure to the ear, but in such a way that the words may be clearly understood by all." Music printing was at first too expensive to alter seriously the social structure of musical performance; the traditions of ostentation and exclusiveness embodied in music written by Guillaume Dufay for the early 15th-century Burgundian court were continued in the magnificent musical establishments of the Italian Renaissance princes and popes. Detailed records exist of the elaborate musical festivities arranged for weddings and baptisms of the powerful Florentine family, the Medici. Printing increased the dissemination as well as the survival of these works; but, like the earlier Burgundian chanson and unlike the contemporary Parisian chanson, which was cast in a more popular mould, they were nonetheless primarily intended for a select group of discriminating performers.

Printing, both of music and of books, does document the ever-increasing development and sophistication of instrumental music during the 16th century. Printed descriptions of instruments date from the 16th century. Their discussions of tuning and technique supplied the needs of professional and nonprofessional musicians alike. There was a growing tendency to construct instruments in families (whole consorts of homogeneous timbre, high, middle, and low), a tendency perhaps related to recent expansion at both ends of the musical scale: with more space available, contrapuntal parts no longer crossed so frequently and no longer needed the differentiation provided by the markedly contrasting timbres of the medieval "broken consort."

THE 17TH AND 18TH CENTURIES

After printing, the next significant influence on music performance was the gradual emergence of the audience, for the relationship between participants in the musical experience—between performer and listener—became polarized. The first evidence for this shift was the rise of the professional vocal virtuoso about the last quarter of the 16th century, and this development soon had a profound influence on musical style. Italian composer-singers, such as Giulio Caccini and Jacopo Peri, reacted quickly to their audiences' desire for more expressive and passionate vocalism, and the music they wrote for themselves eventually was imitated and refined by other composers, such as the Italian Claudio

Monteverdi, whose nine successive books of madrigals document the changes in style from music composed for four to six essentially equal voices to music in which the interest lay primarily at the extremes of the texture. The technical underpinning for this new monodic style was the basso continuo, or thorough bass, played by one or more polyphonic solo instruments "realizing" a "figured bass": that is to say, improvising chords above a single line of music provided with numbers and other symbols to indicate the other notes of the chords. In the 17th century a wide variety of continuo instruments was used, including lute, theorbo, harp, harpsichord, and organ. By the 18th century the practice was more standardized: the bass line would be realized on a keyboard instrument and reinforced by a monophonic bass instrument, such as a lute, viola da gamba, cello, or bassoon. The continuo player not only completed the harmony but could also control rhythm and tempo to suit the particular conditions of a performance.

The development of monody was itself a necessary precondition for that most expensive of all performance institutions, opera. Beginning in Florence at the very end of the 16th century, opera soon spread over Italy: through Rome, where its initially pastoral nature matured into full-blown spectacle, to Venice, where the first public opera theatre opened in 1637. There, although audiences were still aristocratic, opera was dependent upon the sale of admissions rather than royal patronage, and musical performance began to find an entirely new method of economic support.

In the realm of purely instrumental music, the new economy of performance was slower to emerge, but there were many other new developments. By far the most popular Renaissance instrument had been the versatile lute; it served all levels from the merchant's daughter learning the simplest dance melody to the virtuoso. In the 17th century the lute began to yield to keyboard instruments, but the intimate music of the French *clavecinistes* (harpsichordists) was still a clear outgrowth of the precious and evanescent performance style of the 17th-century lutenist Denis Gaultier. Later, keyboard ornamentation began to be codified in tables of agrément-symbols published with each new collection of music. In Italy composers also were attempting to provide performers with more explicit directions. Contemporary keyboard fingering systems, which used the thumb much less than modern ones, also served contemporary preference for subtlety and unevenness of rhythm. As the century progressed and national styles drew further apart, there evolved a specifically French tradition of *inégalité*: performing certain evenly written notes unequally, with alternately longer and shorter values.

A more lasting French development was the first instance of instrumental music consistently performed by more than one player to a part. In 1656, Jean-Baptiste Lully made his orchestra, the Petits Violons ("Little Violins"), abandon the old tradition of free embellishment and drilled them in a disciplined and rhythmically pointed precision that was widely imitated. Simultaneously, the violin and its family, because of their passionate brilliance and versatility, replaced viols as the standard ensemble instruments—especially quickly in Italy, where performance was less sophisticated, less mannered, and less restrained than in France.

In the 18th century, national performance styles tended again to merge, except in the case of opera. French opera, which had reached its first height under

Lully and had counted among its star performers Louis XIV himself, continued to emphasize ballet and correct declamation more than pure vocalism. In other areas, standardization and codification were the trend. The place of improvised embellishment and variation was further circumscribed, limited in general to such recognized spots as repeated sections in binary and da capo forms, slow movements of sonatas and concertos, and cadences. Instrumental tutors by famous performers were important and widespread.

The foundation of public concerts increased, and orchestras all over Europe followed the pattern set by the famous ensemble maintained by the elector of the Palatine at Mannheim, with its standard size (about 25) and new style of performance with dramatic dynamic effects and orchestral devices (e.g., crescendos, tremolos, grand pauses). The Mannheim composers also hastened the decline of the improvised thorough bass by writing out harmonic filler parts for the violas; conducting from the keyboard nevertheless remained standard practice into the 19th century. Meanwhile, entrepreneurial speculation was finally supplanting aristocratic patronage as the economic base for concert activity. Joseph Haydn, who had already spent one full career in Austria, in the service of the House of Esterházy, in 1791 began another and more lucrative one in association with the concert manager Johann Peter Salomon—conducting his London symphonies from the piano.

THE 19TH CENTURY

The heyday of the concert artist began before Haydn's first journey to London, and it still shows few signs of ending. It reached its zenith and was the primary factor in all music performance in the 19th century. Mozart and Beethoven were famous concert pianists before they were famous composers, and succeeding generations saw a large number of piano virtuosos traveling throughout Europe and, later, North and South America. Some were composers of works for themselves; others were more important as interpreters of other composers' works. The tradition of the star singer was of course much older, and it continued; one new development was that of the claquer, paid by the star for his applause. The independent conductors, as distinct from first violinists or continuo players, emerged from the body of the orchestra during the first half of the 19th century, and the development of conductors as lionized figures of the 20th and 21st centuries was swift. Parallel with this rise came the establishment of many of today's major orchestras: New York Philharmonic (1842), Vienna Philharmonic (1842), Boston Symphony (1881), Berlin Philharmonic (1882), Amsterdam Concertgebouw (1883), Chicago Symphony (1891), and London Symphony (1904).

The result of the enormous widening of concert activity and of the increasingly international reputations of performers was an even further standardization of performance practice. Eighteenth-century concern with appropriateness and taste in embellishment yielded to emphasis on clarity and evenness of touch, purity of intonation, and accuracy of execution. As composers' scores became increasingly precise, the performers' interpretative decisions were increasingly limited to matters of technique, tempo, rhythmic and dynamic nuance and personality—a subjectivism justified by the cult of Romantic genius prevalent in 19th-century artistic life.

Real improvisation in music would not re-emerge until the 20th century—in jazz. The addition of such mechanical aids and improvements as chin rests and end pins to stringed instruments (which permitted a wider and more constant vibrato without tiring); valves and extra keys to brass and woodwind instruments (making scales more even and intonation more secure); and double-escapement action, iron frames, and cross-stringing to the piano (which facilitated crisper and surer attack and made both tone and tuning last longer) all had profound influence not only on performance techniques but also on the very sound of the instruments. The most successful new instrumental and vocal teaching methods emphasized virtuosity, brilliance, evenness, and wide range, reflecting a desire to make music more effective for large audiences.

The rise of the concert artist was seconded by the appearance of the professional music critic, whose influence on performance has been, and is, difficult to assess. At first critics tended to be primarily practicing musicians; later this was less the case. A more tangible residue of 19th-century music performance and one that illustrates how little its basic social structures have changed since then is the large number of concert halls and opera theatres that were built and are still used today.

Fréderic Chopin sits at a piano at the home of his Parisian publisher in 1849. Although he performed in only 30 public concerts, Chopin had a high reputation as a pianist.

One final development, the import of which would not be fully realized until the 20th century, was that of historicism: the active revival of old music. This incipient recognition of the validity of other styles of composition and performance is dated conventionally from the German composer Felix Mendelssohn's 1829 performance of parts of J.S. Bach's *St. Matthew Passion*, but it was preceded in a sense by the Concerts of Antient Music (1776–1848) in London. The stated policy of this musical group was not to perform music less than 20 years old (but they often updated the compositions with added brass parts). The revival of interest in the music of Giovanni Pierluigi da Palestrina and Bach, while at first expressed only in terms of 19th-century Romanticism, would pave the way for 20th-century advances and retrenchments in both style and performance.

THE 20TH CENTURY AND BEYOND

The major performing institutions of the 19th century have continued into the 21st century with only minimum structural change, except for a rather belated movement toward unionization of personnel; this development has of course improved the performers' lot greatly, while increasing the costs of performance. Unquestionably, the major new influence on 20th-century music performance was electronics. Broadcasting and recording widened even further the potential audience for concert artists, at the same time as they tended to decrease the physical necessity for large new public performance arenas. Electronic instruments appeared, both amplified versions of older ones (guitar, piano, and even some woodwinds) and instruments with fundamentally electronic means of tone production (electronic pianos and organs, the theremin and Ondes Martenot, sound synthesizers, and still later developments). Other new compositional and performance possibilities also emerged—for example, film, tape, stereophonism, and computers. Even before the phonograph (invented c. 1875) had begun to be regarded as more than a toy, serious research into the authentic performance of older music had produced an awareness of possibilities that pointed the way out of late Romantic gigantism and subjectivism. From the very beginning of the 20th century, the chamber concerts given by Arnold Dolmetsch and his family, on reconstructions of old gambas and recorders, attracted attention to small ensembles and different sonorities and encouraged the activities of other artists.

The true end of the Romantic era and the beginning of the modern era can be dated from the second decade of the 20th century, the time of the composition of two masterpieces that more than any others mark the departure from 19th-century performance ideas: the German composer Arnold Schoenberg's *Pierrot Lunaire* (1912) and the Russian composer Igor Stravinsky's *Histoire du soldat* (1918; *The Soldier's Tale*). These are chamber works, but their instrumental makeup is a unique mixture of instruments that do not necessarily blend and that seem further to repudiate the orchestra as a performing medium. *Pierrot* is a series of songs that repudiate the 19th-century lied: the voice does not sing but produces a kind of pitched speech (*Sprechstimme*). *Histoire* repudiates both orchestra and opera as previously understood: it is specifically (and inexpensively) designed for performance on a portable stage by three dancers, a narrator, and seven instrumentalists. For these works a new kind of performer was required, and these works in turn helped to train the new performer—who might be called the group-virtuoso. Teams or groups of such performers subsequently sprang up everywhere. Often centred on a living composer or the university where he or she taught, they essentially functioned as partners in the compositional process, realizing the work rather than interpreting it. Such performers were very much involved in the creative act, the product of which reflected their particular skills and personalities, and the dynamics of the working situation. Among the most influential composers of the 21st century has been John Adams, known for blending diverse musical genres—including

The Yale in New York concert series presented Igor Stravinsky's *The Soldier's Tale* in 2014. The concert suite was scored for the roles of a reader, the devil, the princess (a dancer), and the soldier, and seven instruments (a clarinet, a bassoon, a cornet, a trombone, a violin, a double-bass, and percussion).

jazz, pop, and electronic music—in his works as well as assembling vocal texts from popular media, government documents, personal interviews, and other sources.

Since the mid-20th century the established performance situation has moved from the formal, ritualized event of the past to a more informal and spontaneous type of gathering. The interaction of various media has led to new art forms and circumstances. Many artists have attempted to create performance situations that actively involve as participants all those in attendance. In such compositions, the roles of composer, performer, and listener are consolidated in a single participant, who in interaction with others arrives at an art work, which all have invented, realized, and perceived, and which can never take place in exactly the same way again. On the other hand, the ever-increasing use of technology has intensified the problem of evaluating the meaning and effect of electronically produced and assembled performances that, in their totality, never took place at all and possibly never could.

The electronic media continue to improve so that anyone may be able to select chamber, concert, opera, and other new types of performance from anywhere in the world, experiencing them through nearly lifelike reproduction facilities. Vast numbers of people may study performance skills via two-way transmission with great artists. The number of actual public performing events may decrease as private musical performance increases. Already there is the phenomenon of the widespread dissemination of great performers' recordings, which has forced the standards of quality for a live performance to almost inhuman heights and has increased interest in the performance of older as well as contemporary music.

JOHN ADAMS

John Adams (born 1947) is an American composer and conductor whose works have been among the most performed of contemporary classical music.

Adams became proficient on the clarinet at an early age (sometimes freelancing with the Boston Symphony Orchestra and performing with other groups) and by his teenage years was composing. His teachers at Harvard University (A.B., 1969; M.A., 1971) included Leon Kirchner and Roger Sessions. Adams was the first Harvard student to be allowed to submit a musical composition as a senior honours thesis. After graduation he moved to California, where from 1972 to 1982 he taught at the San Francisco Conservatory of Music. In 1978 he founded and directed the San Francisco Symphony Orchestra's series "New and Unusual Music," and he was composer-in-residence with the orchestra from 1982 to 1985. From 2003 through 2007 he held the composer's chair at Carnegie Hall in New York City, where he founded the eclectic and diverse "In Your Ear" festival. Increasingly as his career developed, he conducted performances of music by himself and by others, working with organizations such as the Chicago Symphony Orchestra, the Cleveland Orchestra, the Concertgebouw Orchestra (Amsterdam), and the London Symphony Orchestra.

Although his early compositions were in an academic style, Adams soon began drawing on much broader sources, including pop, jazz, electronic music, and minimalism. His use of minimalist techniques—characterized by repetition and simplicity—came to be tempered by expressive, even neo-Romantic, elements. His works encompass a wide range of genres and include *Shaker Loops* (1978), chamber music for string septet; *Harmonium* (1980), a cantata for chorus and orchestra using the poetry of John Donne and Emily Dickinson; *Grand Pianola Music* (1981–82), a reworking of early 20th-century American popular music for instrumental ensemble, three sopranos, and two pianos; *Harmonielehre* (1984–85), for orchestra, an homage to Arnold Schoenberg, whose music was the antithesis of minimalism; and *Wound-Dresser* (1988), for baritone and orchestra, a work based on Walt Whitman's poems about his experience as a nurse in the American Civil War. One of Adams's especially popular orchestral works was the fanfare *Short Ride in a Fast Machine* (1986). The recording of another popular orchestral work, *El Dorado* (1991), won a 1997 Grammy Award. Later

(CONTINUED ON THE NEXT PAGE)

(CONTINUED FROM THE PREVIOUS PAGE)

large-scale works include the *Violin Concerto* (1993) and *My Father Knew Charles Ives* (2003), for orchestra, which alludes to Ives's works and compositional methods.

Adams's most ambitious works, however, were his operas. The first two were created in collaboration with the director Peter Sellars, the poet Alice Goodman, and the choreographer Mark Morris. *Nixon in China* (1987) took as its subject the visit of U.S. Pres. Richard M. Nixon to China in 1972. *The Death of Klinghoffer* (1991) was based on the hijacking by Palestinian terror- ists of the cruise ship *Achille Lauro* in 1985 and the killing of a disabled Jewish passenger. The composer's third opera, *Doctor Atomic* (2005), was the story of the scientists in Los Alamos, New Mexico., U.S., who during World War II devised the first atomic bomb.

In a departure from his 2005 statement that "if opera is actually going to be a part of our lives…it has to deal with contemporary topics," Adams based his fourth opera, *A Flowering Tree* (2006), on South Indian folktales; again Sellars was his collaborator. The work was created in homage to Mozart, taking as its inspiration *The Magic Flute* (1791).

Adams's operas have been regularly per- formed, and they have been recorded; *Nixon in China* won a 1988 Grammy Award. A number of critics have found them to be among the most significant of contemporary operas. Adams created orchestral and choral works from his opera scores, including *The Nixon Tapes* (1987), for voices and orchestra, and *Doctor Atomic Symphony* (2005). *The Chairman Dances*, subtitled "Foxtrot for Orchestra," which was written for *Nixon in China* but dropped from the final score, became one of Adams's most-often-played orchestral works.

After the terrorist attacks of Sept. 11, 2001, the New York Philharmonic Orchestra and Lincoln Center for the Performing Arts in New York City commissioned a work from Adams: *On the Transmigration of Souls*, for orchestra, chorus, children's choir, and prerecorded sound track, first performed Sept. 19, 2002. The text of the work derived from three sources: fragments from notices posted at the World Trade Center site by friends and relatives of the missing, interviews published in the *New York Times*, and randomly chosen names of victims. For this composition Adams was awarded the 2003 Pulitzer Prize in music; the recording won three 2004 Grammy Awards.

Adams has received numerous other honours and awards as well. He was elected to the American Academy of Arts and Letters in 1997. Also in 1997 he was named Composer of the Year by the venerable magazine *Musical America*. A festival in his honour at Lincoln Center in April and May of 2003 was the most extensive single-composer festival that had ever been held there.

(*CONTINUED ON THE NEXT PAGE*)

(CONTINUED FROM THE PREVIOUS PAGE)

Adams's more recent works include *City Noir* (2009) and *Scheherazade.2* (2015). *City Noir* has been described as symphonic jazz. *Scheherazade.2*, a dramatic symphony that harkens to the classic *One Thousand and One Nights*, is a commentary on the mistreatment of women.

EXPRESSION

In European music before the 19th century, as in jazz and much non-Western music, the performer's responsibility included not only the nuances but also often the notes themselves. Thus, in much 17th- and 18th-century music, the composer notated only the main structural notes of the solo part, leaving the performer to improvise ornamental figuration. He was expected to introduce specific ornaments, such as trills and slides, and in many cases to modify substantially the notated rhythm. Similarly, the accompanist, provided only with a thorough bass, an accompaniment notated only as a bass melody line and figures signifying chords, was expected to supply the accompaniment in the correct style. Clues to this correct style ranged from the title of the piece to the tempo indication to the kinds of note values employed.

Instructions for the speed, or tempo, of a performance have the longest history. As early as the 9th century, plainsong manuscripts had the signs "c" (*celeriter*, "quick") and "t" (*trahere*, "slow"), but such indications were exceptional, for the musical repertory was well known to the performers, and written sources served purely for reference purposes. Only from the 16th century do frequent directions for tempo occur, mostly in collections having a wide variety of musical forms and styles, e.g., the vihuela (guitar-shaped lute) publications of the Spaniard Luis Milán or the lute books of the German Hans Neusidler. Such early, often long-winded directions led to later, more methodical indications of tempo, achieved at first by defining the type of piece. Thus, "pavane" indicated a type of dance but also that the piece was to be played in a stately and subdued fashion. In the 18th century other dance titles, such as allemande, gavotte, and courante, gave precise information as to speed and style of performance. The 17th century saw the introduction of the Italian terms that have been in use ever since, often imprecise in meaning, but running roughly hierarchically from slow to fast as follows: adagissimo, adagio, lento, andante, andantino, allegretto, allegro, presto, prestissimo.

Dynamics are expressed more simply and directly. The Venetian Giovanni Gabrieli (1556?–1612) introduced the words piano (soft) and forte (loud) into his scores; they became the basis of a system running from pianissimo (*pp*) to fortissimo (*ff*), with softer and louder extensions possible. Sforzato (*sfz*) means a sudden sharp accent, and sforzando (*sf*), a slight modification of this. Increases and decreases in loudness are indicated graphically as < and > but can also be written as crescendo (*cresc.*) and diminuendo (*dim.*).

More technical instructions, although often in Italian, frequently appear in some other language. These include directives for the insertion or removal of mutes (*con sordino*; *senza sordino*), the retuning of a string (*scordatura*), raising the bell of a wind instrument into the air (usually in German music, *Schalltrichter auf!*), and other actions.

The expression of nuance and feeling is immensely difficult to indicate directly. *Mit Empfindung* ("sensitively"), *espressivo*, and *expressif* appear in abundance in late 19th-century scores and are usually self-explanatory. Although many composers, particularly in the 20th and 21st centuries, put indications of expression into their scores in their own languages, Italian remains the dominant language for such indications, if only because it has provided an international vocabulary taught to the musician along with the basic principles of notation.

MUSICAL STYLES AND GENRES IN WESTERN MUSIC

All ancient civilizations entered historical times with a flourishing musical culture. That the earliest writers explained it in terms of legend and myth strongly suggests the remote beginnings of the art of sound. Among the speculations about its origin, the more plausible are that it began as a primitive form of communication, that it grew out of a device to expedite communal labour, or that it originated as a powerful adjunct to religious ceremonies. While such theories must necessarily remain speculative, it is clear, despite the prehistoric musical artifacts found in central Europe, that the cradle of Western music was the Fertile Crescent cupping the eastern end of the Mediterranean Sea. There the Mesopotamian, Egyptian, and Hebrew nations, among others, evolved political, social cultures that were absorbed by the conquering Greeks and, in turn, by the Romans, who introduced elements of that Mediterranean music to much of western Europe.

In all of these early cultures the social functions of music were essentially the same, since their climate, geographic location, cultural pace, and mutual influences produced many more social similarities than differences. The primary function of music was apparently religious, ranging from heightening the effect of "magic" to ennobling liturgies. The other musical occasions depicted in both pictures and written accounts were equally functional: stirring incitements to military zeal, soothing accompaniments to communal or solitary labour, heightening aids to dramatic spectacles, and enlivening backgrounds to social gatherings that involved either singing or dancing or both. In every case musical sounds were an adjunct either to bodily movement (dance, march, game, or work) or to song. Many centuries were to pass before pleasure in euphonious sound became an end in itself.

THE ESTABLISHMENT OF WESTERN MUSICAL TRADITIONS

Western musical traditions can be traced back to their roots in antiquity, the Middle Ages, and the Renaissance.

ROOTS IN ANTIQUITY

Into the 21st century, ghosts of ancient civilizations are plainly audible in Western music. The essential modes of modern music (Ionian, Dorian, Phrygian, etc.) originated in ancient Greece. Instruments that were played as long ago as five millennia were not unlike some of those used in performance today.

ANCIENT MIDDLE EAST AND EGYPT

The inhabitants of the Mesopotamian region around the Tigris and Euphrates rivers—the Sumerians, the Babylonians, and the Assyrians—flourished from about

3500 to about 500 BCE. Their pictures and the few surviving artifacts indicate that they had instruments of every basic type: idiophones, whose sound is made by resonating as a whole; aerophones, which resonate a column of blown air; chordophones, with strings to be plucked or struck; and membranophones, made of stretched skins over a resonating body. An undecipherable hymn engraved in stone, dating from about 800 BCE, is evidence of a primitive system of musical notation.

The Egyptians, entering historical times about 500 years later than the Mesopotamians, enjoyed all of the same types of activities and instruments, as may be deduced from numerous written references to music as well as seen on many artifacts, especially the pictures preserved on pottery utensils.

The musical culture of the Hebrew peoples, recorded from about 2000 BCE and documented primarily in the Hebrew Bible (Old Testament), was more directly influential in the West because of its adoption and adaptation into the Christian liturgy. Because of the prohibition of Jewish religious law against the making of "graven images," there are very few surviving artifacts or pictures. Among the established practices of the temple service still current in the synagogue are the extensive use of the shofar (a ritualistic ram's-horn trumpet) and the singing of passages from the Torah (Pentateuch; the first five books of the Bible), prayers, and songs of praise.

ANCIENT GREECE

Of the eastern Mediterranean cultures, it was undoubtedly that of the Greeks that furnished the most direct link with the musical development of western Europe, by way of the Romans, who defeated them but adopted much of Greek culture intact. Entering historical times relatively late, circa 1000 BCE, the Greeks soon dominated their neighbours and absorbed many elements of earlier cultures, which they modified and combined

A detail from a Greek *kylix*, a drinking cup, c. 520–510 BCE, shows an *auloi* player with a *phorbeia* (a leather strap tied across the cheeks for additional blowing support) and dancer with *krotala* (castanets).

into an enlightened and sophisticated civilization. The two basic Greek religious cults—one devoted to Apollo, the other to Dionysus—became the prototypes for the two aesthetic poles, classical and romantic, that have contended throughout Western cultural history. The Apollonians were characterized by objectivity of expression, simplicity, and clarity, and their favoured instrument was the kithara, a type of lyre. The Dionysians, on the other hand, preferred the reed-blown *aulos* and were identified by subjectivity, emotional abandon, and sensuality.

The prevailing doctrine of ethos, as explained by ancient Greek philosophers such as Plato and Aristotle, was based on the belief that music has a direct effect upon the soul and actions of humankind. As a result, the Greek political and social systems were intertwined with music, which had a primary role in the dramas of Aeschylus, Sophocles, Euripides, and Aristophanes. And the Grecian educational system was focused upon *musica* and *gymnastica*, the former referring to all cultural and intellectual studies, as distinguished from those related to physical training.

To support its fundamental role in society, an intricate scientific rationale of music evolved, encompassing tuning, instruments, modes (melodic formulas based on certain scales), and rhythms. The 6th-century-BCE philosopher and mathematician Pythagoras was the first to record the vibratory ratios that established the series of notes still used in Western music. From the total gamut of notes used were derived the various modes bearing the names of Grecian tribes—Dorian, Phrygian, Lydian, etc. The rhythmic system, deriving from poetry, was based on long–short relationships rather than strong–weak accentual metre. After

Pythagoras, Aristoxenus was the major historian and theoretician of Greek music.

ANCIENT ROME

When the musical culture of the eastern Mediterranean was transplanted into the western Mediterranean by the returning Roman legions, it was inevitably modified by local tastes and traditions. In most cases, the resulting practices were more limited than their models. The diatonic (seven-note) scale, for example, became the standard, displacing the chromatic and enharmonic structures of the Grecian system. Of particular consequence was the new concept of metre as a series of equal durations, with emphasis being determined by accent (stress) rather than by duration.

An inventory of the musical heritage transplanted from the ancient East (particularly Greece) to Rome reveals the rich treasure inherited: an acoustical theory that accounted for the identification and classification of tones; a concept of tonal organization resulting in the system of modes; principles of rhythmic organization; basic principles of instrument construction; a system of notation that conveyed all necessary indications of pitch and duration; and a large repertory of melodies to serve as models for further composition.

THE MIDDLE AGES

With the decline of the Roman Empire (5th century CE), the institution destined to perpetuate and expand the musical heritage of antiquity was the Christian church, but it was not a unified process.

MONOPHONIC LITURGICAL CHANT

Many of the cultural centres of the Western church developed distinctive characteristics while sharing the common heritage of the Hebrew liturgy and Greek culture. In Milan, for example, metrical hymnody, as distinguished from the earlier practice of unmetred psalmody, was cultivated, particularly under the influence of the 4th-century bishop Ambrose, who first attempted to codify the growing repertory of chants. This body of Milanese church music, therefore, came to be called Ambrosian chant. Somewhat later a unique style and repertory known as Mozarabic chant evolved in Spain, and in France the Gallican style prevailed.

But the mainstream of church music was the type of chant practiced in Rome. Beginning in the late 6th century, according to tradition, with Pope Gregory I, the vast number of traditional melodies that became the foundation for the later development of Western art music were codified and organized. A systematic organization of tonal materials also was gradually accomplished, resulting in the eight church modes. Each melody was assigned a specific function in the services of the liturgical year—some for the mass and some for the divine offices such as matins, vespers, and compline. After a period of assimilation, the Gregorian chant repertory began a process of expansion in the 9th century, when the practice of troping originated. A trope is either a text or a melodic section added to a preexisting melody or a combination of text and music incorporated into existing liturgical music. It is not surprising that church musicians, after years of singing traditional chants, should want to express themselves by adding words to vocalized melodies. Perhaps the motive was more functional:

the added syllables would make the long textless passages easier to remember. Tuotilo (died 915), a monk of Sankt Gallen (in what is now Switzerland), is credited with the invention of tropes. Notker Balbulus (died 912) is notable for his association with the sequence, a long hymn that originated as a trope added to the final syllable of the Alleluia of the mass.

DEVELOPMENT OF POLYPHONY

At the same time that the Gregorian repertory was being expanded by the interpolation of tropes and sequences, it was being further enriched by a revolutionary concept destined to give a new direction to the art of sound for hundreds of years. This concept was polyphony, the simultaneous sounding of two or more melodic lines. The practice emerged gradually during the early Middle Ages, and the lack of definite knowledge regarding its origin has brought forward several plausible theories: it resulted from singers with different natural vocal ranges singing at their most-comfortable pitch levels; it was a practice of organists adopted by singers; or it came about when the repetition of a melody at a different pitch level was sung simultaneously with the original statement of the melody. Whatever motivated this dramatic departure from traditional monophony (music consisting of a single voice part), it was an established practice when it was described in *Musica enchiriadis* (c. 900), a manual for singers and one of the major musical documents of the Middle Ages. To a given plainsong (or *vox principalis*), a second voice (*vox organalis*) could be added at the interval (distance between notes) of a fourth or fifth (four or five steps) below. Music so performed was known as organum. While it may be assumed that the first attempts at polyphony involved only parallel motion at a set interval, the *Musica enchiriadis* describes and gives examples of two-part singing in similar (but not exactly parallel) and contrary movement—evidence that a considerable process of evolution had already taken place.

The next major source of information was the *Micrologus*, written in the early 11th century by the Italian monk and musical theorist Guido d'Arezzo. That work documented principles that were crucial to the further development of polyphony. Rhythmic independence was added to melodic independence, and the added voice might sing two or more tones to one in the original plainsong. During the half century after Guido's death, developments came more rapidly as the plainsong chant became the lower rather than the upper voice. After the emancipation of the organal part, *vox organalis*, its ultimate freedom was reached in the organums of the monastery of Saint-Martial in Limoges, France, where the plainsong part was reduced to the role of sustaining each tone while the organal part indulged in free melismata (groups of notes sung to a single syllable), either improvised or composed. This new style was called *organum purum*.

THE NOTRE-DAME SCHOOL

Early in the 12th century the centre of musical activity shifted to the church of Notre-Dame in Paris, where the French composer Léonin recorded in the *Magnus Liber Organi* ("Great Book of Organum") a collection of two-part organums for the entire church year. A generation later his successor, Pérotin, edited and revised the *Magnus Liber*, incorporating the rhythmic patterns already well known in secular music and adding more than one part to the cantus firmus (the "given" or pre-existing plainsong melody). When metre was applied to the original plainsong as well as to the *vox organalis*, the resulting form was called a clausula. Then, when words were provided for the added part or parts, a clausula became a motet. At first the words given to the motet were a commentary in Latin on the text of the original plainsong tenor (the voice part "holding" the cantus firmus; from Latin *tenere*, "to hold"). Later in the 13th century the added words were in French and secular in nature. Finally, each added part was given its own text, resulting in the classic Paris motet: a three-part composition consisting of a portion of plainchant (tenor) overlaid with two faster moving parts, each with its own secular text in French. At the same time another polyphonic form, the conductus, was flourishing. It differed from a motet in that its basic part was not plainsong and that all parts sang the same Latin text in note-against-note style. The conductus gradually disappeared with the rise of the motet, which apparently served both liturgical and secular functions.

ARS NOVA

When the influential treatise *Ars Nova* ("New Art") by the composer Philippe de Vitry appeared early in the 14th century, the preceding epoch acquired its designation of *Ars Antiqua* ("Old Art"), for it was only in retrospect that the rapid developments of the century and a half from circa 1150 to circa 1300 could appear as antiquated. De Vitry recorded the innovations of his day, particularly in the areas of metre and harmony.

While 13th-century music had been organized around the triple "modal" rhythms derived from secular music and a harmonic vocabulary based on "perfect" consonances (unison, fourth, fifth, octave), the New Art of the 14th century used duple as well as triple divisions of the basic pulse and brought about a taste for harmonious intervals of thirds and sixths.

The musical centre of 14th-century Italy was Florence, where a blind organist, Francisco Landini, and his predecessors and contemporaries Giovanni da Cascia, Jacopo da Bologna, and Lorenzo and Ghirardello da Firenze were the leading composers of several new forms: madrigals (contrapuntal compositions for several voices), ballatas (similar to the French virelai), and caccias (three-voice songs using melodic imitation).

MONOPHONIC SECULAR SONG

Secular music undoubtedly flourished during the early Middle Ages, but, aside from sporadic references, the earliest accounts of such music in the Western world described the music of the goliards—itinerant minor clerics and students who, from the 7th century on, roamed the land singing and playing topical songs dealing with love, war, famine, and other issues of the day. The emergence in France of a fully developed secular musical tradition about the beginning of the 12th century is evidence that the art had been evolving continuously before that time. Partially motivated by the attitude of chivalry engendered by the Crusades, a new lifestyle began among the nobility of southern France. Calling themselves *troubadours*, they circulated among the leading courts of the region, devoting themselves to writing and singing poetry in the vernacular. The troubadour movement flourished in Provence during the 12th and 13th centuries. About the middle of the 12th century, noblemen of northern France, most notably Adam de La Halle, took up the pastime, calling themselves trouvères. In Germany a similar group known as minnesingers, represented by Walther von der Vogelweide, began their activities about 1150 and continued for almost a century after their French counterparts had ceased composing. Late in the 13th century the burgher class in Germany began imitating the aristocratic minnesingers. Calling themselves Meistersingers, they flourished for more than 500 years, organizing themselves into fraternities and following strict rules of poetry, music, and performance. The most famous of them, Hans Sachs, was immortalized in the 19th century in Richard Wagner's opera *Die Meistersinger von Nürnberg*. Relatively little is known of similar secular musical activities in Italy, Spain, and England. Closely associated with the entertainments of the aristocratic dilettantes were the professional musicians of the peasant class called jongleurs and minstrels in France, *Gaukler* in Germany, and scops and gleemen in England.

The musical style that had been established by the troubadours—which was monophonic, of limited range, and sectional in structure—was adopted by each of the succeeding groups. Of particular significance in view of its influence on polyphonic music was the metric system, which is based on six rhythmic modes. Supposedly derived from Greek poetic metres such as trochaic (long–short) and iambic (short–long), these modes brought about a prevailing triple metre in

French music, while German poetry produced duple as well as triple metre. A great variety of formal patterns evolved, in which musical structure and poetic structure were closely related. The most characteristic was the ballade, which was called Bar form in Germany, with an AAB structure. This type, along with the rondeau (song for solo voice with choral refrain) and the similar virelai (an analogue of the Italian ballata), was destined to become a favoured form employed by composers of polyphony such as Guillaume de Machaut, the universally acknowledged master of French music of the Ars Nova period. Machaut also continued the composition of motets, organizing them around recurrent rhythmic patterns (isorhythm), a major structural technique of the age. The beginnings of an independent instrumental repertory during the 13th century are represented by the estampie, a monophonic dance form almost identical in style to the vocal secular music.

THE RENAISSANCE PERIOD

The term Renaissance, in spite of its various connotations, is difficult to apply to music. Borrowed from the visual arts and literature, the term is meaningful primarily as a chronological designation. Some historians date the beginning of the musical Renaissance to about 1400, some to the rise of imitative counterpoint about 1450. Others relate it to the musical association with humanistic poetry at the beginning of the 16th century, and still others reserve the term for the conscious attempt to recreate and imitate supposedly classical models that took place about 1600.

THE COURT OF BURGUNDY

No one line of demarcation is completely satisfactory, but, adhering to commonly accepted usage, one may conveniently accept as the beginning of the musical Renaissance the flourishing and secularization of music at the beginning of the 15th century, particularly at the court of Burgundy. Certainly, many manifestations of a cultural renaissance were evident at the time: interest in preserving artifacts and literature of classical antiquity, the waning authority and influence of the church, the waxing humanism, the burgeoning of urban centres and universities, and the growing economic affluence of the states of western Europe.

As one manifestation of their cultivation of elegant living, the aristocracy of both church and state vied with one another in maintaining resident musicians who could serve both chapel and banqueting hall. The frequent interchange of these musicians accounts for the rapid dissemination of new musical techniques and tastes. Partly because of economic advantages, Burgundy and its capital, Dijon, became the centre of European activity in music as well as the intellectual and artistic focus of northern Europe during the first half of the 15th century. Comprising most of eastern France and the Low Countries, the courts of Philip the Good and Charles the Bold attracted the leading musicians of western Europe. Prime among them was Guillaume Dufay, who had spent some time in Rome and Florence before settling in Cambrai about 1440. An important contemporary of Dufay was Gilles Binchois, who served at Dijon from about 1430 until 1460. The alliance of Burgundy with England accounted for the presence on the Continent of the English composer John Dunstable, who had a profound influence on Dufay. While the contributions of the English to the mainstream of Continental music are sparsely documented, the differences in style between Dufay and his predecessor Machaut are partially accounted for by the new techniques and, especially, the richer harmonies adopted by the Burgundian composers from their English allies.

The social circumstances of the age determined that composers would devote their efforts to the mass, the motet, and the chanson (secular French song). During the first half of the 15th century, the mass became established as a unified polyphonic setting of the five main parts of the Ordinary of the mass (Kyrie, Gloria, Credo, Sanctus, Agnus Dei), with each movement based on either the relevant portion of plainsong or, reflecting the dawning Renaissance, a secular song such as the popular "L'Homme armé" ("The Armed Man") and "Se la face ay pale" ("If my face seems pale"). Still reflecting medieval practices, the preexisting melody (cantus firmus) was usually in the tenor (lowest) part and in long, sustained tones, while the upper parts provided free elaboration. Dufay's nine complete settings of the mass, compared with Machaut's single setting, give a clear indication of the growing importance of the mass as a musical form. The motet became simply a setting of a Latin text from Scriptures or the liturgy in the prevailing polyphonic style of the time. It was no longer necessarily anchored to a plainsong tenor; the composer could give free reign to his invention, although some did, of course, resort to older techniques.

It was in secular music that giant strides took place. While their chansons continued the tradition of rondeaux, virelais, and ballades, Dufay and his contemporaries added free forms divorced from the ordered patterns of the Ars Antiqua and Ars Nova periods.

Among the distinctive features of Burgundian musical style was the prevailing three-part texture, with melodic and rhythmic interest centred in the top part. Because it was so typical of secular songs, this texture is commonly referred to as "ballade style" whether it appears in mass, motet, or chanson. Its possible stylistic implication is that a solo voice sang the upper melody, accompanied by instruments playing the lower parts, although no documents remain to establish exactly how the music was performed. There was probably no standard performing medium: all parts may have been sung; some or all may have been doubled by instruments; or there may have been one vocal part supported by instrumental accompaniment.

THE FRANCO-FLEMISH SCHOOL

A watershed in the history of music occurred about the middle of the 15th century. The fall of Constantinople (now Istanbul) in 1453 and the end of the Hundred Years' War at about the same time increased commerce from the East and affluence in the West. Most significant musically was the pervasive influence of musicians from the Low Countries, whose domination of the musical scene during the last half of the 15th century is reflected in the period designations the Netherlands school and the Franco-Flemish school. These musicians traveled and resided throughout Europe in response to their great demand at princely courts, including those of the Medici family in Florence and the Sforzas in Milan. Further dissemination of knowledge resulted from the invention and development of printing.

The leading composers, whose patrons were now members of the civil aristocracy as well as princes of the church, were Jean de Ockeghem, Jakob Obrecht, and, especially, Josquin des Prez. Ockeghem, born and trained in Flanders, spent most of his life in the service of the kings of France and was recognized by his contemporaries as the "Prince of Music." Obrecht remained near his birthplace in the Netherlands, going occasionally to Italy in the retinue of Duke Ercole I of Ferrara. More typical of the peripatetic Netherlanders was the career of Josquin, the most-influential composer of the period. After training at Saint-Quentin, he served the Sforza family in Milan, the papal choir in Rome, Ercole I, and King Louis XII of France before returning to his native Flanders in 1516. These three composers and several contemporaries hastened the development of the musical techniques that became the basis of 16th-century practice and influenced succeeding developments.

Flemish composer Jean de Ockeghem (with glasses), in a detail of a manuscript miniature from the late 15th century.

Rather than the three parts typical of most Burgundian music, four parts became standard for vocal polyphony in the late 15th century. The fourth part was added below the tenor, increasing the total range and resulting in greater breadth of sound. The presence of the four parts also allowed for contrasts of texture such as the "duet style" so characteristic of Josquin, when the two upper parts might sing a passage alone and be echoed by the two lower parts alone. The emergence of the technique of imitation (one voice repeating recognizably a figure heard first in another voice) as the chief form-generating principle brought about more equality of parts. At the same time, "familiar style," in which all parts move together in chords, provided a means of textural contrast. The great variety of rhythmic techniques that evolved during the 14th and early 15th centuries made possible a wide range of expression—from quiet tranquility for sacred music to lively and spirited secular music. Knowledge of the musical practices comes not only from the thousands of surviving compositions but from informative treatises such as the 12 by the composer Johannes Tinctoris (1436–1511), one of which, *Terminorum musicae diffinitorium* (c. 1475), is the earliest printed dictionary of musical terms.

The chief forms of vocal music continued to be the mass, the motet, and the chanson, to which must be added other national types that developed during the 15th century—the villancico (secular poetry set for voice and lute or for three or four voices) in Spain and the frottola (a simple, chordal setting in three or four parts of an Italian text) in Italy. The emergence of the frottola in northern Italy led to the development of the Renaissance madrigal, which impelled that country to musical supremacy in Europe.

INSTRUMENTAL MUSIC

At the same time, an independent instrumental idiom was evolving. While instruments had been in common usage throughout the Middle Ages, their function was primarily to double or to substitute for voices in vocal polyphonic music or to provide music for dancing. Techniques unsuitable for voices were doubtless part of an instrumentalist's musical vocabulary, but most such music was improvised rather than being written. Although there are a few sources of instrumental music dating from the 13th and 14th centuries, the earliest relatively extensive documentation comes from the 15th century, particularly from German sources, such as the *Buxheimer Orgelbuch* and Conrad Paumann's *Fundamentum organisandi* (*Fundamentals of Organ Playing*). The compositions in both collections are of two basic types, arrangements of vocal works and keyboard pieces entitled *Praeambulum* (*Prelude*).

During the course of the 16th century, instrumental music burgeoned rapidly, along with the continually developing idiomatically instrumental techniques, such as strongly accented rhythms, rapid repeated tones and figures, angular melodic lines involving wide intervallic skips, wide ranges, long, sustained tones and phrases, and much melodic ornamentation.

Dance forms, a continuation of a tradition unbroken since the beginnings of recorded music history, were most characteristically composed in pairs, although single dances as well as embryonic suites of three or more dances appeared. The pairs usually consisted of pieces in contrasting tempo and metre that often were unified by sharing a common melody. Common dance pairs included the pavane and galliard, the allemande and courante, and the basse danse and tourdion.

Preludes continued as a major form of organ music and were joined by the fantasia, the *intonazione*, and the toccata in a category frequently referred to as "free forms" because of the inconsistency and unpredict-ability of their structure and musical content—sections in imitative counterpoint, sections of sustained chords, sections in virtuoso figuration. If a distinction must be made, it might be said in very general terms that the fantasia tended to be more contrapuntal while the toccata ("touch piece") featured passages designed to demonstrate the performer's agility, although the designations were freely interchangeable. To the same category belong the descriptive pieces such as *The King's Hunt*, which featured naive musical representa-tions of natural sounds.

The ricercare and the canzona, generally referred to as fugal forms because of their relationship to the principle of the fugue (that of melodic imitation), arose out of the growing understanding of and dependence on imitation as a unifying structural technique. Although these designations were applied to a great variety of pieces—some identical in style to the fantasia or pre-lude—the classic ricercare of the 16th century was virtually an instrumental motet, slow and churchlike in character and consisting of a number of sections, each utilizing imitation. The canzona followed the same structural principle but was a lively counterpart to the chanson, with the sections sometimes in contrasting tempo and metre. Cantus firmus compositions were based upon preexisting melody. During the 16th century most were designed for liturgical usage but were based upon both secular melodies and plainsong. In most cases the cantus firmus was sounded in long, sustained tones while the other part or parts added decorative contrapuntal lines. The organ mass, in which the choir and the organ alternated lines of the liturgical text, was a popular practice.

Variations also often used a preexisting melody but differed from cantus firmus compositions in that the melody was much shorter and was repeated a number of times, each time with different accompanying parts. The two basic types during the Renaissance were the plain, or melodic, variations and the ground. In the former, the chosen melody usually appeared in the top part and was varied in each repetition with ornamentation and melodic figuration or with changing accompaniments. The ground, or ground bass, was a simple melodic pattern sounded in the lowest part, which served as a foundation for imaginative figuration in the upper parts.

The four major vehicles for instrumental music of the period were the lute, the organ, stringed keyboard instruments, and instrumental ensembles. Most popular by far was the lute, which could produce the major elements of instrumental style except for long, sustained tones. Noteworthy composers of lute music included Luis Milán in Spain, Arnold Schlick in Germany, and John Dowland in England. The organ, because of its close association with liturgical music, continued to be an important instrument, and its literature includes all of the formal types except dances. Among the leading organ composers were the Germans Paumann, Schlick, and Paul Hofhaimer, the Italians Claudio Merulo and Andrea and Giovanni

This English virginal (with the jack rail removed) was made by Robert Hatley in London in 1544.

Gabrieli, the Spaniard Antonio de Cabezón, and the Englishman John Bull.

The two basic classes of stringed keyboard instruments were the harpsichord (virginal, spinet, clavecin, clavicembalo), with quill-plucked strings, and the clavichord, with strings struck by thin metal tongues. Keyboard instruments were highly capable of idiomatically instrumental effects and flourished, particularly in England, from the last half of the 16th century onward, thanks to the composers William Byrd, Bull, and Orlando Gibbons. A major manuscript source of the keyboard works of these masters is the famous *Fitzwilliam Virginal Book* of the 17th century.

Instrumental ensembles of the Renaissance were not standardized, although consorts (groups) of viols, of woodwind instruments such as recorders and shawms (loud oboes), or of brass instruments such as the cornet and sackbut (early trombone) were common. More common, however, were mixed consorts of various types of instruments, depending on the players available. All types of instrumental forms were performed by ensembles except for the prelude and the toccata, which were essentially keyboard works. Representative composers included the Gabrielis and Gibbons.

VOCAL MUSIC IN THE 16TH CENTURY

At the beginning of the 16th century the style of vocal music was generally uniform because of the pervading influence of Netherlanders during the preceding half century. That uniformity persisted well into the late Renaissance but was gradually superseded by emerging national differences, new forms, and the increasing importance of Italy as a musical centre during the last half of the 16th century.

The rapid accumulation of new musical techniques and resources produced a wide vocabulary of artistic expression, and the invention of music printing helped the rapid dispersal of new techniques. In an age in which music was an essential social grace, composers wrote more secular music, in which fewer technical restrictions were in force and experimentation and novelty were applauded. Advances were particularly apparent in venturesome harmonies as chromaticism (the use of notes not belonging to the mode of the composition) sounded the death knell of the modal system.

Liturgical practice dictated that the mass and the motet remain the chief forms of sacred vocal music. Compared with secular music, their style was conservative, but inevitably some of the newer secular techniques crept in and figured effectively in the music of the Counter-Reformation within the Roman Catholic Church.

Four distinct types of mass settings were established during the century. Two types were continuations of earlier practice: the tenor mass, in which the same cantus firmus served for all five portions of the Ordinary of the mass, and the plainsong mass, in which the cantus firmus (usually a corresponding section of plainsong) differed for each portion. Reflecting the more liberal attitudes of the Renaissance were the free mass, with no borrowed materials, and the parody mass, in which the entire polyphonic web was freely adapted from a motet or a secular composition. In all cases when a cantus firmus was used, the preexistent melody might appear in its original form or in paraphrased version, with tones added, omitted, or altered. As a result of the upheaval in the church caused by the Reformation, new forms derived from established models appeared in Protestant worship: the German Lutheran chorale (hymn tune, arranged from plainsong or a secular melody), the chorale motet, English anthems (Anglican form of motet) and services, and the psalm tunes in Calvinist areas.

While not young in a chronological sense, the musical life of Italy was reborn at the beginning of the 16th century after a century of relative dormancy. The frottola remained the prevailing secular form in northern Italy for the first three decades of the century.

When the humanistic poets, seeking a more-refined expression, and the Netherlanders and composers trained by them, applying a more-sophisticated musical technique, turned their efforts to the frottola, the result was the madrigal. The name was borrowed from the 14th-century form, but there was no resemblance in poetic or musical structure. Compared with the frottola, the earliest Renaissance madrigals, dating from about 1530, were characterized by quiet and restrained expression. Usually written for three or four voices, they were mostly homophonic (melody supported by chords) with occasional bits of imitation. Among the early madrigal composers were several Flemish composers resident in Italy, among them Adriaan Willaert, Jacques Arcadelt, and Philippe Verdelot. About 1560 the normal number of parts increased to five or six, and the texture became more consistently polyphonic. At the same time, more attention was given to expressive settings of the text, notably in the madrigals of Cipriano de Rore, Philippe de Monte, and the Gabrielis. During the last two decades of the century and continuing until the middle of the 17th century, the musical style of the madrigal changed appreciably. The late madrigals were of a very dramatic nature, featuring colouristic effects, vivid word-painting, and extensive chromaticism. Their declamatory character dictated a return to a more homophonic style. Noteworthy among the many composers of the late madrigal were Luca Marenzio, Carlo Gesualdo, and Claudio Monteverdi.

During the course of the century, simpler secular forms, such as the villanella, the canzonetta, and the balletto, appeared in Italy, largely as a reaction against the refinement, complication, and sophistication of the madrigal. They reverted to the chordal style of the frottola, often with intentionally parodistic lyrics. The balletto was particularly distinguished by a refrain of nonsense syllables such as "fa la la."

Most of the Italian forms, along with their designations, were adopted by Elizabethan England during the last half of the 16th century. Most leading English composers, from William Byrd and Thomas Morley to John Wilbye, Thomas Weelkes, and Orlando Gibbons, contributed to the vast treasury of English secular music. Morley is particularly important as the editor of the most-significant collection of English madrigals, the *Triumphes of Oriana*, published in 1603 and dedicated to Queen Elizabeth I (Oriana). These pieces correspond in style roughly to the middle-period Italian madrigal. English counterparts of the canzonetta and balletto were the canzonet and ballett. A late 16th-century innovation in both Italy and England was the ayre (air), a simple chordal setting especially suitable for a solo voice with a lute or a consort of instruments playing the other parts. John Dowland and Thomas Campion were notable composers of ayres.

The French counterpart of Italian and English madrigals was the polyphonic chanson, a continuation of the chief medieval and early Renaissance form of secular music. Revitalized by composers such as Josquin, Clément Janequin, and Claudin de Sermisy, the chanson developed several distinctive features: a clearly delineated sectional structure with some repetition of sections, much vivid programmatic writing, and occasional use of irregular metric organization. The irregular metric structure, called *musique mesurée*, was used for maintaining faithfully the accentuation of the poetry and reflects the traditional primacy of textual over musical considerations in French music.

The lied, or song, continued its 15th-century role as the chief secular form in Germanic areas, but it did not develop to the same extent as the madrigal and the chanson. Throughout the Renaissance it was relatively conservative in its adherence to the cantus firmus principle and its tendency toward chordal over contrapuntal texture. Following Heinrich Isaac in the 15th century, the major 16th-century lieder composers were Ludwig Senfl, Hans Leo Hassler, and Johann Hermann Schein. To all national schools of the 16th century must be added the name of the Flemish composer Orlando di Lasso, who wrote in French, Italian, or German, depending on his current employment. The Spanish villancico was a flourishing popular form, but there was no Iberian equivalent to the madrigal, the chanson, or the lied.

THE TONAL ERA AND AFTER: 1600 TO THE PRESENT

The beginning of the 17th century was one of the most dramatic turning points in the history of music, even more so than the beginning of the Ars Nova and almost as revolutionary as the beginning of the 20th century. The winds of change had been felt several decades earlier, and the establishment of the new style required several decades after the turn of the century, but the year 1600 saw the performance of several works destined to change the course of music.

THE BAROQUE ERA

Originally used in a derogatory sense of referring to something bizarre, degenerate, and abnormal, the term Baroque gradually acquired a positive connotation for the grandiose, dramatic, energetic spirit in art that prevailed during the period from about 1600 to about 1750. The new spirit required a vastly expanded musical vocabulary, and a rapid evolution of new techniques occurred, particularly in vocal music. Two distinct musical styles were recognized. One, the *prima prattica* (or *stile antico*), was the universal style of the 16th century, the culmination of two centuries of adherence to Flemish models. The other, called *seconda prattica*, or *stile moderno*, referred to the new theatrical style emanating from Italy.

The expanded vocabulary allowed for a clearer distinction between sacred and secular music as well as between vocal and instrumental idioms, and national differences became more pronounced. The tonal organization of music evolved also, as the medieval modes that had previously served as the basis of melody and harmony were gradually replaced, during the 17th century, by the system of tonality dominating Western music until about 1900: a system based on contrasting keys, or sets of interrelated notes and chords deriving from a major or minor scale. Viewing the period as a whole, two additional innovations most clearly distinguish it from the preceding Renaissance: concertato, or the contrast, combination, and alternation of voices and instruments, and basso continuo (thorough bass, figured bass), an accompaniment consisting of a low-pitched instrument, such as a violoncello or a bassoon, combined with a keyboard instrument or lute capable of harmonic elaboration.

OPERA

Most typical of the emerging style were the dramatic productions of the Camerata, a group in Florence who were dedicated to recreating and imitating the musical ideals and practices of classical antiquity—in a sense, the musical manifestation of the Renaissance. Their guiding philosophy was the preeminence of textual over musical considerations; their belief was that the function of music was to heighten the dramatic impact of words. The musical result was monody: originally recitative (solo singing reflecting speech rhythms), later also arioso (more lyric than recitative) and aria (more elaborate song), accompanied by a basso continuo that could provide an innocuous background to a solo voice. Among the major figures in this revolutionary movement were Giulio Caccini and Jacopo Peri, both of whom composed operas based on the legend of Orpheus and Eurydice. Caccini also provided the name for the new movement with his publication of *Le nuove musiche*, a collection of solo songs with continuo accompaniment. The ideas and techniques conceived by the Camerata spread rapidly over Italy and, subsequently, all over Europe.

During the 1620s and 1630s the centre of operatic activity shifted from Florence to Rome, where several distinctive features developed: a chorus was used extensively, dancing was incorporated into the dramatic spectacle, and an overture in the style of a canzona became the accepted norm. A flourishing operatic activity developed a decade later in Venice, where the first public opera house was opened in 1637. Public taste began to influence operatic composition, and, as a result, several innovations, such as the extensive use of popular tunes, spectacular staging, and short, fanfare-like overtures, were introduced. The audience's desire for tuneful songs also contributed to the clear distinction between recitative and aria, which began with the Venetian school. Foremost among contemporary composers was Monteverdi, who had known of the activities of the Florentine Camerata while serving as musical director to the Gonzaga family in nearby Mantua. He adopted the new style for his later madrigals and wrote two operas, *Orfeo* (1607) and *L'Arianna* (1608), before moving to Venice in 1613. Francesco Cavalli and Antonio Cesti became the leading Venetian operatic composers after Monteverdi's death in 1643.

The last major operatic centre to develop in Italy began its activities in the 1670s in Naples. Neapolitan *opera seria*, or serious opera, with characters from classical history or mythology, dominated Europe for a century. It was essentially a series of recitatives and arias, the latter mostly of the da capo type (ABA, the A section given improvised embellishment on its repetition) characterized by florid virtuosic singing. Other features were, first, the distinction between recitativo secco (dry recitative), accompanied by the continuo, and recitativo accompagnato, or stromentato, accompanied by the orchestra, and, second, the establishment of the Italian overture. Called a sinfonia, the overture in three parts (fast–slow–fast)

Italian composer Alessandro Scarlatti, pictured here in 1692, wrote operas and religious works. He established the form of the Italian overture, a forerunner of the classical symphony.

evolved into the symphony during the 18th century. Alessandro Scarlatti was the most influential of the early Neapolitan operatic composers.

During the same period, opera was introduced at courtly functions outside Italy. After Luigi Rossi's *Orfeo* was performed in Paris in 1647, the Italian form was gradually merged with the major French dramatic form, the ballet; the importance of dancing in French operas thereafter is not surprising. Another distinguishing feature was the French overture (a slow movement, a fast movement, and, occasionally, a return to the opening slow section), which, like the Italian overture, later had an independent life. The masters of French opera during the Baroque period were Jean-Baptiste Lully and his successor Jean-Philippe Rameau. Because of the social and political upheaval of the Thirty Years' War, there was less operatic activity in Germany than in France, and the activity that did occur was more completely dominated by the Italian style. Hamburg, Munich, Dresden, and Vienna were the major centres, with Reinhard Keiser and Georg Philipp Telemann as the most prolific composers.

The situation in England resembled that in France, since the English also had a flourishing musicodramatic form, the masque, which gradually merged with Italian opera. Henry Purcell and John Blow were the chief composers of opera in English before Italian domination of serious opera became almost complete during the 18th century.

CANTATA AND ORATORIO

The leading Neapolitan opera composers also helped to establish the Baroque successor to the madrigal—the cantata—which originated as a secular form for solo voice with instrumental accompaniment. Giacomo Carissimi standardized the form as a short drama in verse consisting of two or more arias with their preceding recitatives. The cantata was introduced into France by one of Carissimi's students, Marc-Antoine Charpentier; Louis Nicolas Clérambault continued the tradition in the late Baroque period. With the fading stylistic distinction between sacred and secular music, the cantata was quickly converted to church purposes, particularly in Germany, where it became the chief decorative service music for the Lutheran Church. Dietrich Buxtehude and Johann Kuhnau were two of the leading composers of such church cantatas.

While the new concertato techniques were being applied to established forms of church music, such as the mass, service, motet, anthem, and chorale, new forms emerged that were clear departures from Renaissance styles and types. The oratorio and settings of the Passion story developed simultaneously with opera and on almost identical lines, consisting of recitatives, arias, vocal ensembles, instrumental interludes, and choruses. Emilio del Cavaliere was the "founder" of the oratorio with his *La rappresentazione di anima e di corpo* (*The Representation of the Soul and the Body*). Produced in Rome in 1600, this work, unlike true oratorio, used actors and costumes. Carissimi and Alessandro Scarlatti were the chief Italian Baroque composers of oratorio, and Heinrich Schütz, a pupil of both Giovanni Gabrieli and Monteverdi in Venice, was the leading 17th-century German composer in this field.

INSTRUMENTAL MUSIC

The new techniques of *Le nuove musiche* were to be heard in music for instruments, especially now that they participated in genres formerly written for unaccompanied voices (e.g., the motet). The forms and mediums of instrumental music remained essentially the same but with considerably different emphasis. The lute, for example, lost status quickly with the rise of the harpsichord as the most common instrument for continuo accompaniment of dramatic productions. The organ, as the traditional church instrument, retained its position and assimilated the evolving forms.

Dance pairs of the Renaissance grew, about the middle of the 17th century, into dance suites consisting basically of four dances: allemande, courante, saraband, and gigue, with optional dances such as the gavotte, the bourrée, and the minuet sometimes inserted before the final movement. Variation forms—the chaconne (in which a set of harmonies or a bass theme is continuously repeated), the passacaglia (in which the theme is repeated but not necessarily in the bass), along with the ground bass and variations on well-known melodies—continued to be popular. Free forms also continued in the patterns of their Renaissance antecedents, while growing in dimension and inventiveness. The toccata, prelude, and fantasia were expanded into multisectional forms using the three basic instrumental textures—imitative counterpoint, chordal homophony, and virtuosic passage work—in combination, alternation, and contrast. The Renaissance fugal forms, chiefly the canzona and the ricercar, gradually evolved into the late Baroque fugue, and cantus firmus compositions continued to flourish as a result of their liturgical function.

The major new categories of instrumental music during the Baroque period were the sonata and the concerto. Originally applied to instrumental ensemble pieces derived from the canzona, the term sonata became the designation for a form that was to dominate instrumental music from the mid-18th until the 20th century. In its keyboard manifestation, it was a binary (two-part) structure similar to a dance-suite movement. For small ensemble, it evolved into a series of independent movements (usually in a slow–fast–slow–fast arrangement) called a *sonata da chiesa* ("church sonata") or a dance suite called a *sonata da camera* ("chamber sonata"). Especially prominent was the trio sonata, for two violins (or flutes or oboes) and cello with continuo. Eventually, similar forms were adopted for orchestra (sinfonia or concerto), for orchestra with a small group of featured instruments (concerto grosso), or for a solo instrument with orchestra (solo concerto). The fundamental principle of the concerto was that of contrast of instrumental groups and musical textures.

Throughout the period, keyboard music flourished, notably in the hands of Jan Pieterszoon Sweelinck in the Netherlands, Johann Pachelbel and Johann Froberger in Germany, Girolamo Frescobaldi in Italy, and Domenico Scarlatti in Spain; in France the chief exponents included Rameau and François Couperin.

Instrumental ensemble music, both chamber and orchestral, was dominated by Italians, chiefly from Bologna, the Bolognese school producing such composers as Arcangelo Corelli, Antonio Vivaldi, and Giuseppe Tartini. Purcell in England and Couperin and Jean-Marie Leclair in France are representative of the many composers in other nations who were influenced by Italian models of instrumental ensemble music.

THE LATE BAROQUE

The Baroque era reached its zenith in the work of Johann Sebastian Bach (1685–1750) and George Frideric Handel (1685–1759). Both were born in the same part of Germany; both were reared in the Lutheran Church; and both were primarily organists; but because of different environmental circumstances each became a master of different musical forms. Handel, because of his conditioning in Italy, was primarily a dramatic composer, writing opera, oratorio, and secular cantatas, mostly after he reached England. He also wrote quite extensively for orchestra and instrumental ensemble. Bach, by contrast, was influenced by his life-long employment in the church and by his dedication as a teacher; his works thus include Passions, cantatas for church services, liturgical organ pieces, and harpsichord compositions, many instructional in purpose.

German-English composer George Frideric Handel wrote operas, oratorios, and instrumental compositions. His *Messiah* (1741) is the most famous of all oratorios.

In the works of both Handel and Bach changes in technique reached a culmination with the clear establishment of the tonal system, allowing for modulation from one key centre to another, primarily as a device for formal organization. Rich, chromatic harmonic language was both reason and result of such a change. The fusion of contrapuntal technique with homophonic style resulted in a distinctive hybrid texture that employed figured bass (homophony) as a foundation for two or more independent melodic lines (polyphony).

THE CLASSICAL PERIOD

As in the case of the Renaissance, difficulties with terminology again arise with the label classical. Does it refer to a period of time, a distinctive musical style, an aesthetic attitude, an ideal standard, or an established norm? Again, the term was borrowed from the visual arts of the same epoch and is awkward when applied to music in that there were no known models from classical antiquity for composers to imitate. A full understanding of the term depends on a clear conception of the term romantic, for the two stand at opposite poles. Each represents a set of artistic ideals that has been in opposition to the other since both were recognized by early Grecian writers. As has been noted, the ancient Greek followers of Apollo established the ideal of classicism, whereas the cult of Dionysus produced the prototype of romanticism. A mixture of the two qualities has prevailed throughout recorded history, with first one and then the other in the ascendancy. Thus, there have been many "classic" and many "romantic" eras, but the labels have come to refer most specifically to the last half of the 18th century and the 19th century, respectively, because those periods represent most vividly the two tempers.

The social and political scene during the late 18th century was hardly a setting for a quiet, composed "classical" age in view of the prevailing revolutionary spirit and colonial rivalry. The revolutionary movement did have a direct effect on music in that "music for the masses" became a new ideal—music directly appealing to a large number of unsophisticated people who had previously been excluded from courtly entertainments.

PRECURSORS OF THE CLASSICAL STYLE

As the pendulum swung from the predominantly romantic Baroque period toward the Classical period, there was an inevitable overlapping of the old and the new. While Bach was composing his intricate and erudite polyphony, his sons were reflecting a new ideal, the Rococo. Fostered by the court of the French king Louis XV, whose lifestyle was far less formal than that of his illustrious great grandfather, the Rococo ideal was artistic expression dedicated to elegance, frivolity, and gracefulness; a work of art must be delicate, playful, entertaining, and immediately appealing. The result was often artificial and unrealistic, but it succeeded in capturing the discreetly sentimental and hedonistic attitudes of the times. Powdered wigs, lace cuffs, and perfumed handkerchiefs for both sexes were other manifestations of the same playful spirit that produced music in the *style galant*.

The German counterpart of the essentially French Rococo was the *empfindsamer Stil*, or "sentimental style," which flourished in the 1750s and 1760s. Its leading exponent was one of J.S. Bach's sons, Carl

Philip Emanuel Bach, who served for a time at the court of Frederick the Great in Berlin. The distinguishing feature of this German reaction against Baroque profundity was its concern with emotional feeling in the music itself, on the part of the performers and, hopefully, in the reaction of the audience. The French obsession with lightness, gracefulness, and decoration was countered by the German determination to affect sensibilities that were often more attuned to tears than to laughter. A late and less reserved manifestation of *Empfindsamkeit* was the *Sturm und Drang* ("storm and stress") movement in the arts during the 1770s and 1780s. The inclination toward the more intense personal expression of that movement was a harbinger of the coming Romantic period.

CONSOLIDATION OF THE CLASSICAL STYLE

The fundamental changes in musical style that distinguished Classical from Baroque were inspired by Rococo ideals and refined and stabilized by the Classicists, particularly Joseph Haydn, Wolfgang Amadeus Mozart, Christoph Willibald Gluck, and the young Ludwig van Beethoven.

For the first time in the history of music, instrumental music became more important than vocal music. The orchestra and chamber groups, such as the string quartet, trio, and quintet, and the piano trio became standardized and replaced the heterogeneous trio sonata and other ensembles of the Baroque period. The basic duple and triple organization of metre remained unchanged, but rhythmic patterns tending toward more regularity and simplicity became the rule, producing the

A Mozart family portrait, c. 1780–81, includes Wolfgang Amadeus Mozart (*seated at the piano*) with his sister Maria Anna (*left*), his father, and a portrait of his mother. Mozart is often considered the greatest musical genius of all time.

"tyranny of the bar line" that was to prevail for more than a century.

Melody was inclined to be more motivistic, tuneful, and epigrammatic, in contrast to the extended, figurative style of many Baroque melodies. Harmony was second only to melody as a focal element. Harmonic patterns that clearly established the tonal centre were the rule of the day.

As a reaction against the intricate polyphony of the later Baroque period, homophonic texture dominated by melody became the norm, but the accompanying patterns were different from those of the early Baroque, when monody supported by sustained chords was the prevailing style. In the late 18th century, figurations such as the Alberti bass (form of accompanying figure consisting of broken chords) and rhythmically enlivened repeated chords formed the typical textural patterns. Counterpoint was retained in some forms, however, and regained status particularly in development sections of works in sonata form.

Formal structure, a definitive aspect of classical style, was characterized by simplicity and clarity. Sectional forms (created by contrast and repetition of thematic materials, tonalities, and textures), variations, and the new principle of development (fragmentation, expansion, and modification of themes) were the established norms. Phrases of musical material became shorter and more clearly demarcated as well as more balanced and regular. A new concept of dynamic contrast also contributed to formal clarity. Shading from loud to soft or vice versa provided a dramatic means of building toward an expressive climax. Orchestration and instrumentation were closely allied to dynamic variation, and much more colour contrast and variety appeared in orchestral music, even though the ensemble was more standardized than formerly.

The pattern that served as the structural basis for most instrumental music of the classical period was the sonata. A large-scale work in several movements, it evolved from several Baroque predecessors, chiefly the Italian overture, the *sonata da chiesa*, and the concerto grosso. Depending on the medium of performance for which it was intended, it would be called, for example, a symphony, a concerto, a string quartet, a sextet, a trio. The designation sonata was reserved for a solo instrument or for an instrument accompanied by harpsichord or piano. Originally in three movements, the sonata became standardized as a four-movement form when a minuet was incorporated in the following sequence: (1) a serious allegro, (2) a slow, lyrical movement (andante or adagio), (3) a minuet and trio, and (4) a brilliant, vivacious finale. The internal structure of the first movement was so uniform that it acquired the designation sonata-allegro form; that is, the form employed in the allegro movement of a sonata, consisting basically of exposition, development, and recapitulation. The slower second movement is less structurally predictable. It is frequently a sectional form (for example, ABA, AABA, ABCA) or a set of variations. It may, even though in a slow tempo, be a sonata-allegro form, illustrating again the inconsistency of musical terminology. The third movement, usually omitted in the concerto and sometimes in other forms, is either a graceful minuet or a scherzo, a lively rhythmic form derived from the minuet. The structural pattern of the minuet had been fixed when it was established as the official court dance by Louis XIV in the mid-17th century. The last movement is frequently a rondo form, in which the principal theme recurs regularly between subordinate themes.

INSTRUMENTAL MUSIC

The most important and influential manifestation of the sonata form was that played by an orchestra—the symphony. During the 17th century the term sinfonia had been used for various kinds of instrumental music. "Sonata" was equally ambiguous. Late in the century, the designation sinfonia began to be confined to the Italian opera overture—a three-movement arrangement, fast–slow–fast. By the mid-18th century, opera overtures were being played independently in concerts. The insertion of the minuet between the last two movements resulted in the prototype of the Classical symphony.

During the waning Baroque period, vigorous advocates of the burgeoning Rococo and *Empfindsamkeit* ideals were active in Milan, Vienna, and Mannheim. In Milan, Giovanni Battista Sammartini began writing his symphonies, some 25 of them, in the 1730s. While employing the continuo of his models, Corelli and Giuseppe Torelli, the bithematic plan for his opening movements foreshadowed the exposition of the Classical symphonies. At about the same time, young composers in Vienna were experimenting with the new genre, thus laying the foundation for the later Viennese masters. The most famous and probably the most influential group was active in Mannheim in the court orchestra of Karl Theodor, the elector of the Palatinate. Their activity began in the 1740s, when Johann Stamitz became leader of the orchestra. His experiments with dynamic techniques—crescendo (increasing in loudness), diminuendo (decreasing in loudness), sforzando (special emphasis)—with homophonic textures featuring the first violins in virtuoso passages and with tremolo and other dramatic effects, became the hallmarks of the Mannheim style and served as models for his son Karl Stamitz and for composers in Vienna. Thanks to the fortuitous presence of certain instrumentalists as well as to benevolent patronage, the basic ensemble of the modern symphony orchestra was gradually established: violins, violas, violoncellos, and double basses; two flutes, two oboes, and two bassoons; two French horns and two tympani. Trumpets were added for festive occasions.

Unlike the symphony, which had its origins in other forms, the Classical concerto grew directly out of the

Baroque solo concerto and resembles it in that it is based on exchange of musical material between solo instrument or instruments and orchestra. While directly derived from the ritornello principle of the Baroque concerto (that of a recurrent musical passage when the soloists are silent), the internal structure of the first movement assimilated the developmental principle of sonata-allegro form. Pietro Locatelli and Giuseppe Tartini are especially notable for their numerous late-Baroque violin concerti.

While music for small instrumental ensembles had flourished for over 200 years previously, the late 18th century witnessed the establishment of chamber music in the modern sense of the term: music in sonata form for a small group of instruments with one player for each part. Replacing the trio sonata of the Baroque period, the most popular classical ensemble was a group of four stringed instruments—two violins, a viola, and a violoncello. Both the group itself and a sonata written for the group were called a string quartet. Among other popular ensembles were the string trio (violin, viola, and violoncello; or two violins and a violoncello) and the piano trio (violin, violoncello, and piano).

The solo keyboard sonata was one of the most vital forms of the period, partly because of the great increase in amateur performers resulting from the newly affluent middle class. The sonatas of Domenico Paradisi, of J.S. Bach's sons, and of Haydn and Mozart reflect the evolution from the one-movement, binary form of the Baroque period to the standard classical three-movement form. A four-movement form did not become popular until the time of Beethoven. A celebrated contemporary of Mozart, Muzio Clementi, composed more than 60 sonatas for the piano alone and half again as many for piano and violin or flute and strongly influenced the style of piano writing.

While the sonata was unquestionably the most important form of instrumental music during the period, several other types were cultivated. For orchestra and chamber ensemble, a suitelike work called variously divertimento, serenade, cassation, or notturno was popular for light entertainment, differing from the more serious symphonies, concerti, and sonatas (which were intended for attentive listening) in that the ensemble of instruments was inconsistent, unpredictable, and often unspecified. The number, types, and arrangements of movements were equally flexible, ranging from three to 10 or more, some in dance forms and others in forms suitable for a sonata. While nonsonata forms for solo instruments (particularly keyboard) occasionally bear these designations, the most popular smaller solo forms were sets of variations, individual dances or marches, fantasies, and small pieces that would have been appropriate as movements of sonatas. For some reason, composition for the organ dwindled drastically after the death of J.S. Bach, in 1750.

VOCAL MUSIC

There was less distinction between Baroque and Classical opera than between instrumental styles of the two periods because opera, with musical interest centred on a solo voice, had been largely melodic-homophonic since its inception. Another reason for the continuity of operatic style throughout the 18th century was the universal domination by the Neapolitan opera seria. Even in Paris, where the Lully-Rameau tradition maintained its vitality, there was an Italian opera theatre.

While there was some effective reform of certain aspects of Neapolitan style that had become decadent and some nationalistic reaction in the field of comic opera, nothing in the nature of serious opera challenged Neapolitan supremacy. As a result, the late 18th century was a period of great vitality in operatic composition.

The distinguishing characteristics of Neapolitan opera seria reveal why it is little known and rarely heard today. It was a very conventionalized form, with artificial and overcomplex plots. There were usually six main characters representing three of each sex, with some of the male and female parts sung by castrati (emasculated male sopranos and contraltos). Each character was allotted a standardized number of arias in fairly standardized succession. Obviously, with such constant interruption of the action, dramatic truth received little if any consideration. The singers and the arias were the focus of the entire production, with little of musical interest in the parlando recitatives (i.e., using speech rhythms), little use of chorus, and little function for the orchestra aside from providing a subordinate accompaniment.

Objections to the decadence and artificiality of the Neapolitan style, which had begun to appear as early as the 1720s, would have been fruitless had not a champion appeared to put suggestions and theories for reform into actual practice. Culminating the movement for reform was Christoph Willibald Gluck, who began his career in the 1740s by writing about 20 operas in the prevailing style. Then, beginning with *Orfeo ed Euridice* in 1762, he attempted to enhance both the dramatic and musical components of opera. Superfluous virtuosity and vocal display were drastically curtailed if not eliminated by providing music that reflected the emotional or dramatic situation. As a result of Gluck's reforms, opera moved toward a classical simplicity of style of which his and Mozart's works were the culmination.

A second challenge to established Neapolitan opera was emerging through comic opera in which the subject matter was light, sentimental, often topical, and satirical, reflecting both the social changes of the period and ridicule of serious opera. The music was engagingly tuneful, easy to perform and to comprehend. Comic opera had appeared during the 17th century but began its independent existence during the first half of the 18th century in Italy, where it was called the opera buffa. The French opéra comique evolved during the same period and was given new impetus by the *guerre des bouffons* ("war of the buffoons") of the early 1750s, when support of the Italian opera buffa company then performing in Paris exceeded that of the French heroic opera of Rameau. In England, ballad opera, beginning with *The Beggar's Opera* in 1728, followed a course of development similar in both period and style to that of the *opéra comique*. German singspiel grew out of translations and imitations of English ballad opera. Models that centred on Vienna adhered to the Italian style and culminated in Mozart's *The Abduction from the Seraglio* and *The Magic Flute*. Yet Mozart also brought the old Italian style to its zenith in *Le Nozze di Figaro* (*The Marriage of Figaro*), *Così fan tutte* (*Thus Do They All*), and *Don Giovanni*.

Aside from opera, secular vocal music was composed for solo voice and chorus. But the production of solo songs and cantatas in other countries could not compare with the growing interest in the German lied, which flourished under C.P.E. Bach and later composers. The most extensive development of secular part-songs took place in England, where numerous catches and glees were written.

Large-scale sacred choral music of the period was strongly influenced by the prevailing operatic style. Except for the text, some passages from oratorios and passions are indistinguishable from an operatic excerpt. But the Handelian tradition combined with the Neapolitan style and culminated in Haydn's two noble oratorios, *The Creation* and *The Seasons*. Liturgical music, such as masses, motets, litanies, psalms, and canticles, also demonstrated that the same composers were writing for both church and theatre. In many instances the style was uniform for the two types, although the chorus naturally played a much greater role in church music.

THE ROMANTIC PERIOD

The beginning of the 19th century witnessed a change of both musical style and aesthetic attitude that has become identified as Romantic. The term romantic originated in German literature of the late 18th century, illustrating once again the overlapping of classical and romantic attitudes and ideals. The Franco-Swiss writer Mme de Staël articulated the new ideals of the movement in 1813 as original, modern, national, popular, derived from the soil, religion, and prevailing social institutions. Obviously, some of these proclaimed romantic ideals and purposes were the same as those of the 18th-century Classicists.

ESTABLISHMENT OF THE ROMANTIC IDIOM

In defining classicism, it was suggested that the distinctive elements of musical romanticism embrace emotionalism, subjectivity, individualism, nationalism, and a preference for a certain type of subject matter. Emotionalism is reflected in the revelation of intensely personal feelings, indeed, the sentimentality that pervades 19th-century music. Subjectivity replaces the formalism of the Classical period, in that impulse and inspiration play a major role in the motivation of both composer and performer, and the listener's response is expected to be more sensory than intellectual. Closely related to subjectivity is the individualism reflected in the highly self-centred expression of composers of the period, as well as by the conviction that a composer's most personal thoughts and feelings are the ultimate artistic message. In contrast to the universality of musical style that prevailed during the 18th century, much 19th-century music is identifiable in terms of national origin. Nationalism—the consciousness of the distinctive features of a nation and the intent to reveal, emphasize, and glorify those features—played a prominent part in Romantic music, partly as a result of social and political developments. The subject matter favoured by Romantic composers is most apparent in vocal music, where words can convey the explicit theme, but instrumental music was also affected by the Romantic attraction to national identification and to remoteness, strangeness, and fantasy, particularly to the fantastic aspects of medieval tales and legends.

During the 19th century, musical techniques and materials were rapidly enriched by new resources, all devoted to the ideal of emotional or dramatic expressiveness. The orchestra, the piano, the solo voice with piano accompaniment, and the opera were the four predominating mediums; chamber and choral music occupied a less central position. Duple and triple divisions of the measure remained the basis of metre, but there were occasional experiments with metric irregularity, and rhythm was recognized as one of the most effective agents of expressiveness in music. Strong rhythmic energy, frequently produced by dotted patterns, provided a vigorous force that could be enhanced by faster and faster tempi. Flaccid patterns in slower tempi provided for the requisite pensive or sorrowful moods.

Melodic style was determined on one hand by the vocal ideal of song, with long, lyric lines. On the other hand, the new idiomatic possibilities of instruments were being exploited. In either case, expressiveness was the governing ideal. Harmonic and tonal elements were gradually expanded during the century, with more chromaticism, enriched sonorities (seventh and ninth chords), and more nonharmonic tones resulting in a more flexible tonal scheme. Tonic and dominant chords (those based on the first and fifth notes of the key), were no longer the secure poles of tonal movement; frequent and remote modulations (changes from one key to another) contributed to the restlessness of key centres. Because musical interest was centred in melody and harmony, texture remained prevailingly homophonic, though counterpoint played a prominent role in developmental sections. Fugues and other imitative forms occurred as a result of studied archaism or for special effect, but the composers' preoccupation with direct and immediate expression led them to neglect the traditional polyphonic forms, with their inherent traditions and restraints.

The Romantic abhorrence of formalism has frequently been exaggerated for the purposes of distinguishing between Classical and Romantic attitudes. Established patterns such as the sonata-allegro and rondo forms were subjected to many modifications and extensions, but musical coherence demands a judicious balance of unity and variety, so most compositions of the 19th century are still fairly clear-cut sectional, variational, or developmental forms. The distinctive new features are largely in the area of emphasis and dimension—symphonies lasting over an hour in contrast to the 20- to 30-minute standard of the Classical period. Instrumental colour and variety, as another aspect of expressiveness, was made possible by a greatly enlarged orchestra and figured prominently in the new sound ideal.

The Janus-like figure who marked the transition from the Classical to the Romantic style was Beethoven, the first composer whose personality and character made a purposeful impact on the types and style of music he composed. Inspired by the revolutionary forces prevailing at the time, he declared himself a free artistic agent, with neither allegiance nor responsibility to any patron. His early works reflected the 18th-century acceptance of providing music on demand, and he applied his craftsmanship to supplying compositions in hope of financial reward.

But in his later works, from about 1820 on, he declared his personal independence and wrote only what his imagination and inspiration dictated, thus establishing individuality, subjectivity, and emotional expression as the standard for Romantic composers. Yet the body of music he produced reflects the tastes of the 18th rather than the 19th century, in that he was attracted more by the absolute forms of instrumental music than by the dramatic and lyrical forms cultivated by the Romanticists. Symphonies, chamber music (particularly string quartets), and piano pieces (including 32 sonatas) far outweigh his one opera, one oratorio, one major mass, and assorted songs and part-songs. His lack of interest in dramatic vocal music reflects the classical side of his nature, though the expressive changes apparent in his instrumental works are evidence of his being the springboard to the Romantic epoch.

OPERA

The opera remained a flourishing medium throughout the 19th century, and Italian opera continued as the dominant type during the first half of the century in the hands of Gioachino Rossini, Vincenzo Bellini, and Gaetano Donizetti. The reforms instigated by Gluck were discernible, but enough of the genre's indigenous Italianate character remained to distinguish it from other national types. The man who, more than any other, personifies Italian opera of the period is Giuseppe Verdi (1813–1901), whose works are still among the most performed. Late in the century, the tendency toward even more realistic and topical

Giuseppe Verdi is acclaimed for his Italian operas, including *Rigoletto* (1851), *Il Trovatore* (1853), *La Traviata* (1853), and *Aida* (1871).

subject matter produced the *verismo* ("realism") school of Ruggiero Leoncavallo, Pietro Mascagni, and Giacomo Puccini.

Meanwhile, German opera developed into the epitome of Romantic subject matter and expressiveness, beginning in 1821 with the performance of *Der Freischütz* (*The Freeshooter*, or, more colloquially, *The Magic Marksman*), by Carl Maria von Weber. Plots based on tales from Teutonic mythology and medieval legend that emphasized the mystical aspects of nature were a distinctive feature of Germanic operas and distinguished them from the more mundane Italianate plots.

Richard Wagner (1813–83) crystallized the German Romantic ideal into the music drama, in which all aspects of the production—drama, music, design, performance—were intended to fuse into a manifestation of pure artistic expression in which no one element predominated over the others, as singing still tended to do in Italian opera. There was no development in Germany after Wagner comparable with the post-Verdi verismo group in Italy. Wagner's innovations—once again a readjustment of dramatic versus musical forces in musical theatre—were the point of departure for most German opera since his time, from Richard Strauss to the present.

In Paris, the operatic centre of the world from late in the 18th century until well into the 19th, native composers were quick to sense the Gluckian changes in Italian opera as well as the new directions in Germany. Beginning with Rossini's *Guillaume Tell* in 1829 and crystallizing in the operas of Giacomo Meyerbeer in the 1830s and '40s, French grand opera emerged as the most opulent and grandiose musico-dramatic spectacle of the first half of the century. During the later 19th century, *opéra comique* and grand opera merged to produce the prevailing French lyric opera. At the same time, *opéra comique* branched off in another direction to produce operettas, which developed into the musical comedies of the 20th century. Indigenous opera appeared in other regions, especially in Russia, Bohemia, and Scandinavia, as a result of nationalistic fervour.

ORCHESTRAL MUSIC

Reaching both a culmination and a turning point in the nine symphonies of Beethoven, orchestral music developed in two directions during the 19th century. On the one hand were composers who, because of their training and temperament, adhered primarily to Classical forms and ideals of absolute music. On the other hand were the composers seeking new realms of dramatic content, colour, and expressiveness. Even for the more conservative group, both the forms and the orchestra itself were greatly expanded during the century, but the total output of works was much smaller than in the

Classical period. Romantic musical vocabulary replaced the Classical language in symphonies, of course, and programmatic content (i.e., an extramusical image or story) was a frequent element.

The more progressive composers cultivated new musical types that represented the tastes and ideals of the Romantic period—the concert overture, the symphonic poem (later called tone poem), the symphonic suite, and symphonic variations. The concert overture, a direct development of overtures to dramatic works, was an attempt to reconcile the old classical demands for form with Romantic desire for programmatic content. It was usually a sonata-allegro form with picturesque themes designed to suggest (with the help of the title) characters, locations, or dramatic situations. Felix Mendelssohn's *Hebrides* overture and Brahms's *Tragic Overture* (completed 1880) are representatives of the genre. The symphonic poem, foreshadowed in Hector Berlioz's *Symphonie fantastique* (completed 1830), was originated by Franz Liszt at midcentury as an orchestral work, usually in one movement, based on an extramusical idea such as a poem or a narrative. The futility of attempting to depict explicit events and attitudes in purely musical terms resulted in the demise of the form early in the 20th century after the many tone poems of Richard Strauss. The symphonic suite was one of three distinct types: (1) an outgrowth of 18th-century dance suites, divertimentos, or serenades, (2) the extension of the symphonic poem into a composite work of several movements of related programmatic nature, or (3) a group of selections from a dramatic work such as a ballet. Rimsky-Korsakov's *Scheherazade* represents the second type, and Tchaikovsky's *Nutcracker Suite* is typical of the third. While variations had appeared as movements of symphonies and concerti since the mid-18th century, they became an independent orchestral form during the last quarter of the 19th century. César Franck's *Variations symphoniques* (1885) is a good example of the type. Popular orchestral pieces, such as the waltzes of Johann Strauss, also flourished.

The mainstream of composers whose orchestral music reflected most clearly their allegiance to Classical forms and models—though conditioned by Romanticism, of course—is represented by Beethoven, Franz Schubert, Robert Schumann, Johannes Brahms, and Anton Bruckner. The more overtly Romantic contingent was centred around Berlioz, Liszt, Gustav Mahler, and Richard Strauss.

A third group, chiefly nationalists who were reacting against Germanic domination of instrumental music as well as reflecting the sociopolitical developments of the era, combined features of both conservative and progressive camps, to which they added national characteristics. While there were manifestations of the movement in countries such as Hungary, Poland, Spain, and England, the most productive and outstanding of those who sought to reflect national distinctiveness were the Russian "Five"—César Cui, Mily Balakirev, Aleksandr Borodin, Modest Mussorgsky, and Nikolay Rimsky-Korsakov—the Bohemians Bedřich Smetana and Antonín Dvořák, and the Scandinavians Edvard Grieg, Carl Nielsen, and Jean Sibelius. French composers such as Camille Saint-Saëns, César Franck, and Vincent d'Indy were motivated by the same impulse of independence, but they could hardly be categorized as nationalists in the same sense as their eastern

Edvard Grieg was a founder of the Norwegian nationalist school of music. Norwegian folk music stirred his imagination in such works as *Peer Gynt* and *Norwegian Peasant Dances*.

European colleagues, since there was less distinctive folk material from which to draw colourful materials and since they had been in the mainstream of musical development all along.

PIANO MUSIC

One of the most popular media of the Romantic era, thanks to the rapid technical development of the instrument, was piano music. Another reason for the popularity of the piano was the growing demand for recreation and entertainment on the part of the newly affluent middle class. In tune with the taste of the times, small pieces of distinctive expressive character (hence, "character pieces") were the most popular type, either as single pieces or as parts of composite works. Stylized dances continued to be popular, but nationalistic types such as the polonaise and mazurka and the novel waltz replaced the staid minuets of the previous era. Sonatas continued to occupy serious composers, and sets of variations continued to flourish. The virtuosity of the violinist Niccolò Paganini and his contemporaries led to many studies, or études, designed to exhibit the performer's dexterity as well as the invention of the composer. Chopin, Schumann, Liszt, and Brahms were the major composers of piano music after Beethoven, but practically all composers of the time contributed to the literature.

SONGS

The vocal counterpart of the keyboard character piece was the solo song with piano accompaniment. With the rise of the German romantic poetry of Goethe,

Schiller, Heine, and others, about the beginning of the 19th century, the German lied ("song") flourished. After 1850, composers of other nations, especially France and Russia, also produced a song literature of universal appeal. A pioneer and certainly the most prolific composer of lieder was Schubert, who in his short life wrote more than 600 songs. His chief successors, in chronological order, were Karl Loewe, Mendelssohn, Schumann, Brahms, Hugo Wolf, and Richard Strauss.

CHAMBER AND CHORAL MUSIC

The great Viennese tradition of chamber music reached its zenith in the works of Beethoven and with the death of Schubert came temporarily to a close. The conciseness, unity, and balance that were basic to the Classical ideal were incompatible with the essence of musical Romanticism. When writing for instruments, the typical Romantic composer was inclined toward the colouristic effects and expressive possibilities of the orchestra. Chamber music continued to be written and performed, of course, but nowhere was it one of the primary interests of composers as it had been during the 18th century. Predictably, the more conservative composers, such as Mendelssohn, Schumann, and Brahms, were the chief composers of chamber music.

While the same musical vocabulary and style had served both church and opera house since the rise of dramatic music, the 19th century witnessed a separation of musical idioms according to function—sacred or secular. Music for use in church was generally conservative, especially after the "rediscovery" of Palestrina and systematic research into the reform of Gregorian chant. On the other hand, cantatas and popular part-songs produced for the many amateur choral societies incorporated as many of the new techniques as could be managed by the singers. There was some fusion of the two idioms in oratorios and in settings of liturgical texts for the concert hall or for special occasions. The requiem mass, with its vividly dramatic content, was attractive to Romantic composers, and Berlioz's and Verdi's settings remain as emotionally telling today as most operas of the period.

MODERN PERIOD

The striking changes in musical style that occurred about 1900 were a turning point in the history of Western music comparable to the dramatic transformation of the early 14th and early 17th centuries. But never before had the change been so rapid, and never before had there been such a diversity of resulting styles.

DIVERSITY OF STYLES

The last decades of the 19th century witnessed what might be termed the diffusion of Romanticism, when significant departures from the current musical vocabulary appeared in the works of some nationalist composers and especially in the Impressionistic style represented in France by Claude Debussy and Maurice Ravel. The amorphous rhythmic patterns, the whole-tone scale, the concept of free relationship of adjacent harmonies, and the kaleidoscopic textures of musical Impressionism were musical manifestations of the aesthetic movements current in painting and literature.

The experimental works of Arnold Schoenberg and Igor Stravinsky about 1910 heralded a new epoch in music. Schoenberg was the pioneer when his adoption of the ideals of the Expressionist movement—like Impressionism an aesthetic development shared by other art forms—resulted in his discarding traditional harmonic concepts of consonance and dissonance and led to the development of atonality and 12-tone technique (in which all 12 tones of the octave are serialized, or given an ordered relationship). Stravinsky's revolutionary style, variously labelled "dynamism," "barbarism," or "primitivism," concentrated on metric imbalance and percussive dissonance and introduced a decade of extreme experimentation that coincided with World War I, a period of major social and political upheaval.

In contrast with Schoenberg's and Stravinsky's experiments during the second decade of the century, another line of demarcation appeared about 1920 with a general return to the aesthetic ideals of the late 18th century. Following the leadership of Stravinsky, Paul Hindemith, Béla Bartók, and Sergey Prokofiev, among others, most prominent composers entered a Neoclassical period characterized by restraint of emotional content; simplification of materials, structures, and textures; a greater attention to craftsmanship; and a revival of concern for linear counterpoint rather than instrumental or harmonic colour. Baroque emphasis on counterpoint and Classical formalism were now clothed in 20th-century melodic, harmonic, rhythmic, tonal, and orchestral idioms. The Expressionist followers of Schoenberg, most notably Alban Berg, continued in their preoccupation with serial techniques.

Neoclassicism continued as the dominant trend throughout the period from about 1920 until World War

II, while many of the experimental techniques introduced during the revolutionary second decade of the century were gradually refined, modified, and assimilated into the accepted musical vocabulary. At the same time, experimentation continued alongside a tenacious conservatism that echoed Romantic ideals and styles. Nationalism also continued to flourish, reaching a level in some countries never achieved during the 19th century.

After World War II the two leading artistic attitudes tended to merge when the followers of Anton von Webern carried serial composition to such a rigorous extreme that its craftsmanship and intellectual orientation suggested Classicism rather than Expressionism. Shortly afterward, Stravinsky, the doyen of the Neoclassical group, began experimenting with serialism. Avant-garde music since that time has begun to employ the techniques made possible by technological developments in electronics.

ADVENT OF ELECTRONIC COMPOSITION

Beginning about 1950, two leading groups began experimenting with electronic music, one in Cologne and the other in Paris. The product of the latter group was referred to as *musique concrète* in acknowledgement of the principle that preexisting, or "concrete," recorded sounds serve as the basis of all sonorities in the finished work. The basic sounds, which may be derived from any source—musical, natural, or mechanical—are modified electronically and arranged in any combination and succession suitable to the composer's purpose. The German group, led by Karlheinz Stockhausen, was concerned with a purer form of the medium in that its basic sounds are electrically generated instead of being recorded from sources external to the electronic apparatus. The two approaches share one connecting link with music of the past: all sounds have pitch, intensity, duration, and quality. All other concepts of musical organization have been discarded, including the necessity of a performer. Electronic compositions exist on a tape (or disc), and can be made audible by a speaker system. The dehumanizing of music has been carried several steps further by the use of mathematics and even of computers to determine the nature of sound materials—either electronic or that produced by more conventional means—and their organization. At the other extreme is aleatory music, in which the performer is allowed to choose the manner and order of presentation of materials specified or simply suggested by the composer.

POPULAR MUSIC

Another result of advances in electronics has been the tremendous growth of popular music during the 20th century. New techniques have made possible high-fidelity reproduction of sound and its widespread and rapid dissemination through radio, phonograph, tape recorder, and television. In addition, some of the instruments used in popular music have incorporated electronic amplification as well as sound production. While there has been a popular music as long as humankind has turned to singing and dancing for diversion and recreation, much of it was folk music and existed only as an oral tradition. But popular music in the modern sense originated in the late 18th century, when ballads made popular in ballad opera and dance music received wide circulation. The same types flourished throughout the 19th century and into the 20th, when a new direction was prompted by the emergence of jazz among blacks in the southern United States. After the original ragtime came jazz proper, swing, bebop, and rock in its numerous manifestations—punk, new wave, etc. Early in the century, the novelty of jazz rhythms and dominance of brass, woodwind, and percussion instruments over strings attracted some serious composers who occasionally incorporated suitable jazz idioms into their works. Since about 1930, the influence has worked in both directions, and popular music has gradually adopted techniques that originated in serious music. Regardless of the interaction of popular and serious music, the popularity of the former is one of the most significant musical developments of the 20th century, especially in view of the widening gulf between the serious composer and the potential audience.

It is impossible to arrive at a complete and objective

THE MARSALIS FAMILY

The Marsalis family is an American family whose members are considered the "first family of jazz," who (particularly brothers Wynton and Branford) had a major impact on jazz in the late 20th and early 21st centuries. The family includes Ellis (b. November 13, 1934, New Orleans, Louisiana, U.S.) and his sons Branford (b. August 26, 1960, Breaux Bridge, Louisiana), Wynton (b. October 18, 1961, New Orleans), Delfeayo (b. July 28, 1965, New Orleans), and Jason (b. March 4, 1977, New Orleans).

(CONTINUED ON THE NEXT PAGE)

(*CONTINUED FROM THE PREVIOUS PAGE*)

Ellis Marsalis began as a tenor saxophonist but switched to piano while in high school. After earning a music degree from Dillard University and serving in the U.S. Marines, he worked for the AFO (All-for-One) record label in the late 1950s, recorded with brothers Nat and Julian ("Cannonball") Adderley in 1962, and was trumpeter Al Hirt's pianist during 1967–70. It was as a jazz educator, however, that he made his greatest mark. In 1974 he began teaching at the New Orleans Center for Creative Arts, where his pupils included Harry Connick, Jr., Terence Blanchard, Donald Harrison, Nicholas Payton, and Kent and Marlon Jordan, as well as his own six sons, four of whom became celebrated musicians. The success of his sons resulted in Ellis's attaining stardom in the 1980s, and he recorded steadily thereafter.

Wynton Marsalis was the first family member to achieve national fame. He was given his first trumpet by Hirt and studied both classical music and jazz. Although he played with Danny Barker's Fairview Baptist Church Band and was featured with the New Orleans Philharmonic at age 14, his early musical jobs were mostly in rhythm-and-blues (R&B) and funk bands. He became devoted to jazz while studying at the Berkshire Music Center, and he later attended the Juilliard School (1979–81), where he was recognized as among the most gifted musicians at the institution. At age 19 Wynton joined Art

The Marsalis family and ensemble performs in a special concert to honour patriarch Ellis Marsalis with a lifetime achievement award at the Duke Ellington Jazz Festival in 2009. From left to right: Eric Revis on bass, Branford Marsalis on sax, Wynton Marsalis on trumpet, Delfeayo Marsalis on trombone, and Jason Marsalis on drums.

Blakey's Jazz Messengers, in which he displayed the influence of trumpeter Freddie Hubbard. He soon began emulating the sound of Miles Davis and toured with former Davis sideman Herbie Hancock in 1982–83 before rejoining Blakey for a brief stint. By age 20 Wynton was the talk of the jazz world. His brilliant technique, his dedication to acoustic jazz (rather than fusion or R&B), and his ability to excel in both jazz and classical music (winning Grammy Awards in

(*CONTINUED ON THE NEXT PAGE*)

(CONTINUED FROM THE PREVIOUS PAGE)

both categories in 1984) generated headlines, and he became the unofficial leader of the "Young Lions"–new players who updated the hard bop tradition.

Wynton led a quintet that included his brother Branford during 1982–85. Pianist Marcus Roberts was a featured player in a later combo that eventually grew to be a septet (and proved to be the best vehicle for Wynton's playing and composing). In 1987 Wynton cofounded the ongoing Jazz at Lincoln Center program and undertook the leadership of the Lincoln Center Jazz Orchestra. In this capacity he became a lightning rod of controversy because of his championing of traditional jazz styles and his dismissal of most musical developments after 1965. Since he developed his own distinctive style in the late 1980s, however, he consistently ranked among jazz's all-time great trumpeters, playing everything from New Orleans jazz and swing to hard bop. In the 1990s he wrote many extended works (such as *Blood on the Fields*, which won the Pulitzer Prize for music in 1997), toured the world extensively, and became a prominent spokesman for jazz and music education.

Branford Marsalis started out playing soprano, alto, and tenor saxophone (although he rarely played alto after the late 1980s) and studied under his father at the New Orleans Center for Creative Arts; he continued his studies at Southern University in Baton Rouge, Louisiana, and at Berklee College of Music in Boston. In 1980 he played with the Art Blakey Big Band, as well as with such jazz luminaries as Lionel Hampton and Clark Terry, before joining brother Wynton as a member of Blakey's Jazz Messengers in 1981–82. Branford was a key member of Wynton's quintet from 1982 to 1985, during which time he also recorded with Miles Davis and Dizzy Gillespie and toured with Herbie Hancock. He had a falling-out with Wynton in 1985 when he joined pop singer Sting's band, but the brothers later reconciled.

A talented saxophonist who has shown the ability to emulate a variety of his predecessors (including John Coltrane, Sonny Rollins, and Jan Garbarek), Branford has primarily led his own groups since 1986, including a quartet with pianist Kenny Kirkland and a mid-1990s hip-hop ensemble called Buckshot LeFonque. He has also recorded soundtracks, acted in films, been the musical director of *The Tonight Show* (1992–95), made guest appearances on many recordings, worked as a talent scout and record producer for the Sony label, and been featured regularly as a radio host on National Public Radio. More flexible than Wynton in his willingness to explore contemporary music, Branford is nevertheless a highly skilled player in the traditional styles.

(CONTINUED ON THE NEXT PAGE)

(CONTINUED FROM THE PREVIOUS PAGE)

Although overshadowed by Wynton and Branford, Delfeayo Marsalis has gradually carved out a significant career for himself as a J.J. Johnson-inspired trombonist. He studied music, producing, and engineering at Berklee College of Music and made his initial reputation as a record producer starting in 1985. As a trombonist, he worked with Ray Charles, Art Blakey, Abdullah Ibrahim, and, most notably, Elvin Jones. He made his recording debut as a leader in 1992.

The youngest member of the Marsalis family, Jason, made a strong impression at age 14 as a drummer on Delfeayo's recordings. Influenced by New Orleans rhythms and the drum work of Tony Williams, Jason was a coleader of the band Los Hombres Calientes in the late 1990s and has also recorded with Marcus Roberts, Marcus Printup, and his father.

The family first performed together in 2001 at a concert honouring Ellis's retirement from the University of New Orleans music faculty and the establishment of a chair in his name. Their first recording together, *The Marsalis Family: A Jazz Celebration*, was released in 2003.

description of a revolutionary movement while it is in progress; only a period of time can provide the necessary perspective. It can be acknowledged, however, that music has never before passed through a more anarchic phase than in the 20th century. The tremendous number and diversity of stylistic distinctions has precluded a characteristic designation for the first half of the century, but one must be forthcoming, for musicians of the future will need the terms modern and contemporary for their own times.

Despite the disproportionate publicity given to the most radical experiments, the majority of leading composers working today continue along the moderate path established in the late 1920s and 1930s. And, if one can rely on the lessons of history, the mainstream of music will continue to absorb those new techniques that contribute to expressiveness and communication while discarding that which is merely novel and sensational, so that music history will remain an evolutionary rather than a revolutionary process.

That music is important to the human race is generally agreed, although some maintain that all of the art forms are luxuries, not necessities. The ancient Greek philosopher Democritus denied any fundamental need for music, asserting that "it arose from the existing superfluity." (This was an ironic assessment, coming from an early thought leader who valued cheerfulness and is known as the "laughing philosopher.") Aristotle added, "It is not easy to determine the nature of music or why anyone should have a knowledge of it."

DJ, musician, and producer ZEDD performs electronic dance music (EDM) during an after-party for a tour featuring Skrillex in 2012.

English poet and playwright John Dryden, writing almost 2,000 years later, suggested why people "should have a knowledge" of music. In one of his poems, he mused, "What passion cannot Music raise and quell?" Victor Hugo remarked, "Music expresses that which cannot be put into words and that which cannot remain silent."

Going forward, it is difficult to predict where musical expression might lead. Futurists observe that digital technology has changed everything: communication, science, finance, work, entertainment, and practically all other facets of life. Its impact on music began to be felt more than half a century ago. Today, digital science is employed in most aspects of music, from instrument construction and tuning to stage presentation to sound recording and mixing. Professional musicians in most genres have come to rely on it. More significantly, it opens the door for everyone—including those who are physically challenged and those who believe they can't sing or play an instrument—to express themselves through music.

chord A combination of tones that blend harmoniously when sounded together.

chromatic scale A musical scale that consists entirely of half steps.

clef A sign placed on the staff in music to show what pitch is represented by each line and space.

composition A literary, musical, or artistic production.

consonance An agreeable combination of correspondence of musical tones or speech sounds; a musical interval included in a major or minor triad and its inversions.

diatonic Any stepwise arrangement of the seven "natural" pitches (scale degrees) forming an octave without altering the established pattern of a key or mode—in particular, the major and natural minor scales.

dissonance Discord; an unresolved musical interval or chord.

harmony Tuneful sound; the combination of simultaneous musical notes in a chord.

improvisation The act of composing, reciting, playing, or singing on the spur of the moment or without planning.

instrumentation The arrangement or composition of music for instruments, especially for a band or orchestra.

key A system of functionally related chords deriving from the major and minor scales, with a central note, called the tonic (or keynote); the tonality of a scale; the tone or pitch of a voice.

madrigal Complex polyphonic unaccompanied vocal piece on a secular text developed especially in the 16th and 17th centuries.

melody The aesthetic product of a given succession of pitches in musical time, implying rhythmically ordered movement from pitch to pitch.

motive A leading phrase or figure that is reproduced and varied throughout the course of a composition or movement.

movement The rhythmic character or quality of a musical composition; a section of a longer piece of music; rhythm; tempo.

orchestration The arranging of music for an orchestra; specifically: the treatment of a composition with regard to the structure, manipulation, compass, and timbre of the orchestral instruments and their effective combination, the proper distribution of the harmony, and the writing of orchestral scores.

pitch The property of tone that is determined by the frequency of the sound waves producing it: highness or lowness of sound; a standard frequency for tuning instruments.

plainsong Also called plainchant, the Gregorian chant, and by extension, other similar religious chants.

polyphony Music consisting of two or more independent but harmonious melodies.

rhythm Flow of sound in music having regular accented beats.

scale A graduated series of tones going up or down in pitch.

sharp A musical note or tone one half step higher than a specified note or tone; to raise in pitch especially be a half step; to sing or play above the proper pitch.

staff Also spelled stave, in the notation of Western music, five parallel horizontal lines that, with a clef, indicate the pich of musical notes.

tempo Rate of speed at which a musical piece or passage is to be played or sung.

timbre Quality of auditory sensations produced by the tone of a sound wave; the tone distinctive of a singing voice or musical instrument.

tone A sound of definite pitch or vibration; quality of vocal or musical sound.

troubadour One of a class of lyric poets and poet-musicians often of knightly rank who flourished from the 11th to the end of the 13th century chiefly in the south of France and the north of Italy and whose major theme was courtly love.

virtuoso A highly skilled musical performer.

GENERAL WORKS ON MUSIC PERFORMANCE, PRACTICE, STYLES, AND MUSICAL FORMS

The best historical accounts of musical forms, styles, and performance practice are to be found in Donald J. Grout, *A History of Western Music* (1960); Gustave Reese, *Music in the Middle Ages* (1940), and *Music in the Renaissance*, rev. ed. (1959); Manfred F. Bukofzer, *Music in the Baroque Era* (1947); Alfred Einstein, *Music in the Romantic Era* (1947); and William W. Austin, *Music in the 20th Century, from Debussy to Stravinsky* (1966). Sir Donald Francis Tovey, *The Forms of Music* (1956), contains informative and engaging short pieces. Robert Schumann, *On Music and Musicians*, ed. by Konrad Wolff (Eng. trans. 1947), is an example of the work by a 19th-century precursor of the phenomenon of the present-day composer-authors who have contributed to aesthetic theory by elucidating their own works and commentating on other composers and on the scene in general. See also Igor Stravinsky, *Poetics of Music in the Form of Six Lessons* (1947); Paul Hindemith, *A Composer's World* (1952); Aaron Copland, *Music and Imagination* (1952). Discussion of music and film may be found in Lewis Jacobs (ed.), *The Emergence of Film Art* (1969). Twelve-tone technique and varieties of serialism deriving from it are treated in Arnold Schoenberg, *Style and Idea* (1950); and René

Leibowitz, *Schoenberg, et son école* (1947; Eng. trans., *Schoenberg and His School*, 1949). Short pieces on electronic music appear often in periodical literature. Harold C. Schonberg, *Facing the Music* (1981), is a collection of performance-oriented articles. See also Carol MacClintock (ed.), *Readings in the History of Music in Performance* (1979).

The best direct and concise account of the issues of performance is Thurston Dart, *The Interpretation of Music* (1954). Other general views of the subject are Frederick Dorian, *The History of Music in Performance: The Art of Musical Interpretation from the Renaissance to Our Day* (1942, reprinted 1981); and Robert Donington, *The Interpretation of Early Music*, 2nd ed. (1965), which, like Dart, includes a bibliography of sources. What bibliographic aids to individual performers exist are given in "Dictionaries and Encyclopedias of Musical Instruments, Makers, and Performers," in Vincent H. Duckles, *Music References and Research Materials: An Annotated Bibliography*, 2nd ed., pp. 40–50 (1967). An extensive bibliography published on the subject is Kary Vinquist and Neal Zaslav (eds.), *Performance Practice: A Bibliography* (1971). Some book-length studies of particular aspects of musical performance are listed below: P. Aldrich, *Rhythm in Seventeenth-Century Italian Monady* (1966); F.T. Arnold, *The Art of Accompaniment from a Thorough-Bass As Practised in the XVIIth and XVIIIth Centuries* (1931); J.H. Barbour, *Tuning and Temperament* (1951); D.D. Boyden, *The History of Violin Playing, from Its Origins to 1761 and Its Relationship to the Violin and Violin Music* (1965); Walter Emery, *Bach's Ornaments*

(1953); R.E.M. Harding, *Origins of Musical Time and Expression* (1938); Wilfrid H. Mellers, "Theory and Practice," in *François Couperin and the French Classical Tradition* (1950); Fritz Rothschild, *The Lost Tradition in Music: Rhythm and Tempo in J.S. Bach's Time* (1953), and *Musical Performance in the Times of Mozart and Beethoven: The Lost Tradition in Music, Part II* (1961); Denis W. Stevens (ed.), *The Art of Ornamentation in the Renaissance and Baroque* (1967), a stereophonic record; Henry Pleasants, *The Great Singers: From the Dawn of Opera to Our Own Time* (1966); and William P. Malm, *Music Cultures of the Pacific, the Near East, and Asia* (1967).

Comprehensive treatments of form in Western music are Hugo Leichtentritt, *Musikalische Formenlehre*, 3rd ed. (1927; Eng. trans., *Musical Form*, 1951); and R.E. Tyndall, *Musical Form* (1964); a shorter treatment is in Grosvenor Cooper, *Learning to Listen* (1957). For form in traditional and non-Western music, see Bruno Nettl, *Folk and Traditional Music of the Western Continents* (1965); *Music in Primitive Culture* (1956); and William P. Malm, *Music Cultures of the Pacific, the Near East and Asia* (1967). See also, generally, the relevant articles in Willi Apel, *Harvard Dictionary of Music*, 2nd ed. rev. (1969), a good source on any musical subject; Donald Jay Grout, *A History of Western Music* (1960), the best general history of music to date; Adam Carse, *The History of Orchestration* (1925, reprinted 1964), a detailed look at the evolution of the orchestra and musical instruments; Nicolas Rimsky-Korsakov, *Principles of Orchestration, with Musical Examples Drawn from His Own Works*, ed. by Maximilian

Steinberg, 1 vol. (1964; originally published in Russian, 1910), still one of the best texts for the serious student; Romain Goldron, *Ancient and Oriental Music* (1968), examples of non-Western music and instruments. Later monographs include David Epstein, *Beyond Orpheus: Studies in Musical Structure* (1979); and Ethan Mordden, *A Guide to Orchestral Music: The Handbook for Non-Musicians* (1980).

MUSICAL COMPOSITION

Because most writings on musical composition were conceived as didactic treatises for would-be composers, their content has virtually no bearing on a better understanding of crucial aesthetic attitudes and mental processes. Instead, depending on the era from which they hail as well as the specific outlook of their authors, such treatises deal for the most part with contrapuntal rules, harmonic laws, and the like. While numerous books of this type appeared through the ages, it was only with the creation of the educational institutions known as conservatories of music, following the lead of the National Conservatory of France established in the last years of the 18th century, that composition became a discipline formally taught and hence requiring comprehensive textbooks, including the theory of form and instrumentation. This profitable need was satisfied by the voluminous activities of 19th-century writers from J.J. Momigny and Anton Reicha to Vincent d'Indy in France and from Heinrich Christoph Koch to Hugo Riemann in Germany. Few of these books were translated into English, and they are of primary interest to the specialist. The following is a selection of easily accessible monographs and documentary collections with emphasis on firsthand testimonies of the creative artists themselves.

Jacques Barzun (ed.), *Pleasures of Music* (1951), a collection of writings about music, including many from the pens of men of literature; Leonard Bernstein, *The Joy of Music* (1959), contains Bernstein's seven "Omnibus" television scripts, including his excellent comments on sketch materials relating to Beethoven's *Fifth Symphony* and its ultimate realization; Frederick Dorian, *The Musical Workshop* (1947), a discussion of various aspects of musical composition, including comments on creative procedures; Hanns Eisler, *Composing for the Films* (1947), rare insights into the problems of cinematographic music from a composer who, during his Hollywood years, tried to turn music into an integral aspect of film art; Max Graf, *From Beethoven to Shostakovich* (1947, reprinted 1969), a popular study of psychological processes involved in composition; Michael Hamburger (ed. and trans.), *Beethoven: Letters, Journals and Conversations* (1960), a concise but well-chosen selection of Beethoven's own words concerning both specific compositions and the problems of the composer in general; Lejaren A. Hiller, Jr., and Leonard M. Isaacson, *Experimental Music* (1959), the first and still basic monograph dealing with the philosophy, procedures, and techniques of composition with an electronic computer; Paul Hindemith, *A Composer's*

World (1961), a leading 20th-century composer looks at various facets of the composer's world, including questions of musical perception, inspiration, technique, performance, and education; Irving Kolodin (ed.), *The Composer as Listener: A Guide to Music* (1958), excerpts from pertinent writings, including letters mostly by important composers of the 19th and early 20th centuries; Edward E. Lowinsky, "Musical Genius: Evolution and Origins of a Concept," *Musical Quarterly*, 50:321–340, 476–495 (1964), excellent documentation of the evolution of a concept that has been associated through the ages more consistently with music than with any other form of artistic production; Alan P. Merriam, *The Anthropology of Music* (1964), a comprehensive treatment of music in relation to culture, drawing upon fieldwork on every continent and at all social levels (see especially ch. 9, "The Process of Composition"); Sam Morgenstern (ed.), *Composers on Music: An Anthology of Composers' Writings from Palestrina to Copland* (1956), an excellent collection, mostly of letters, dealing with general and specific aspects of the composer's work; Ernest Newman, *The Unconscious Beethoven*, rev. ed. (1970), a fascinating, if not unproblematic, study of the successive stages of Beethoen's work as revealed in his sketches by one of Britain's most famous critics; Gertrude Norman and Miriam Lubell Shrifte (eds.), *Letters of Composers: An Anthology, 1603–1945* (1946), one of the most comprehensive of several collections of composers' letters available in paperback; Josef Rufer, *Die Komposition mit zwölf Tönen* (1952, 2nd ed. 1966; Eng. trans., *Composition with Twelve Notes Related to One*

Another, 1965), a cogent introduction to dodeca-
phonic aesthetics and technique by a dedicated
Schoenberg disciple; Arnold Schoenberg, *Style and
Idea* (1950), a discussion of Schoenberg's artistic
motivation and procedures as well as those of the
composers he admired most, including Brahms and
Mahler; Roger Sessions, *The Musical Experience of
Composer, Performer, Listener* (1962), a discussion
of fundamental musical problems by the American
composer; William Oliver Strunk (ed.), *Source
Readings in Music History from Classical Antiquity
Through the Romantic Era* (1950), an indispensable
collection of relevant excerpts from the writings of
philosophers, musical theorists, and composers from
Plato to Richard Wagner; Donald Francis Tovey, *The
Mainstream of Music, and Other Essays* (1961), a
paperback reprint of some of the finest essays by
the great British critic, who discusses basic compositional issues. See also Erich Leinsdorf, *The
Composer's Advocate* (1981).

INSTRUMENTATION

Willi Apel, *Harvard Dictionary of Music*, 2nd ed. rev.
(1969), a good source on any musical subject;
Donald Jay Grout, *A History of Western Music*
(1960), the best general history of music to date;
Adam Carse, *The History of Orchestration* (1925,
reprinted 1964), a detailed look at the evolution
of the orchestra and musical instruments; Nicolas
Rimsky-Korsakov, *Principles of Orchestration, with
Musical Examples Drawn from His Own Works*, ed.
by Maximilian Steinberg, 1 vol. (1964; orig. pub.

in Russian, 1910), still one of the best texts for the serious student; Romain Goldron, *Ancient and Oriental Music* (1968), examples of non-Western music and instruments.

MUSICAL INSTRUMENTS

Comprehensive information on diverse musical instruments is found in such authoritative reference sources as Don Michael Randel, *The New Harvard Dictionary of Music*, 4th ed. (2003); *New Oxford History of Music*, 10 vol. (1954–90), with various reprints and reissues of individual volumes (1976–97); Stanley Sadie (ed.), *The New Grove Dictionary of Musical Instruments*, 3 vol. (1984, reprinted 1997); Bruno Nettl et al. (eds.), *The Garland Encyclopedia of World Music*, 10 vol. (1998–2002); Q. David Bowers, *Encyclopedia of Automatic Musical Instruments* (1972); and Richard Dobson, *A Dictionary of Electronic and Computer Music Technology: Instruments, Terms, Techniques* (1992).

History and evolution of musical instruments are studied in many well-illustrated works, including J. Peter Burkholder, Donald Jay Grout, and Claude V. Palisca, *A History of Western Music*, 7th ed. (2006); Giovanni Comotti, *Music in Greek and Roman Culture* (1989; originally published in Italian, 1979); Thomas J. Mathiesen, *Apollo's Lyre: Greek Music and Music Theory in Antiquity and the Middle Ages* (1999); David Munrow, *Instruments of the Middle Ages and Renaissance* (1976); Sibyl Marcuse, *A Survey of Musical Instruments* (1975); Anthony Baines (ed.),

Musical Instruments Through the Ages, new ed. (1976); Robert Donington, *Music and Its Instruments* (1982); Curt Sachs, *The History of Musical Instruments* (1940, reprinted 1968); and Jeremy Montagu, *The World of Medieval and Renaissance Musical Instruments* (1976), *The World of Baroque and Classical Musical Instruments* (1979), and *The World of Romantic & Modern Musical Instruments* (1981).

Physical properties of the instruments are addressed in Reinhold Banek and Jon Scoville, *Sound Designs: A Handbook of Musical Instrument Building* (1980, reissued 1995); Charles Ford (ed.), *Making Musical Instruments: Strings and Keyboard* (1979); Dennis Waring, *Folk Instruments* (1979, reprinted as *Making Folk Instruments in Wood*, 1982, and as *Making Wood Folk Instruments*, 1990); and Neville H. Fletcher and Thomas D. Rosing, *The Physics of Musical Instruments*, 2nd ed. (1998, reissued 2005).

Exhibitions and collections are the source of useful and well-illustrated information. A selection of catalogs includes Phillip T. Young, *The Look of Music: Rare Musical Instruments, 1500–1900* (1980); Laurence Libin, *American Musical Instruments in The Metropolitan Museum of Art* (1985); James M. Borders, *European and American Wind and Percussion Instruments: Catalogue of the Stearns Collection of Musical Instruments, University of Michigan* (1988); Clifford Bevan, *Musical Instrument Collections in the British Isles* (1990); and James Coover, *Musical Instrument Collections: Catalogues and Cognate Literature* (1981).

Geographic and ethnic distribution of musical instruments is explored in Nicholas Bessaraboff, *Ancient European Musical Instruments* (1941, reissued 1964); Emanuel Winternitz, *Musical Instruments of the Western World* (1967); Jaap Kunst, *Music in Java*, 3rd ed., rev. by E.L. Heins, 2 vol. (1973; originally published in Dutch, 1934); William P. Malm, *Japanese Music and Musical Instruments* (1959, reissued 1990), and *Music Cultures of the Pacific, the Near East, and Asia*, 2nd ed. (1977); S. Bandyopadhyaya, *Musical Instruments of India* (1980); Marie-Thérèse Brincard (ed.), *Sounding Forms: African Musical Instruments* (1989); Mary Remnant, *Musical Instruments of the West* (1978); and Emanuel Winternitz, *Musical Instruments and Their Symbolism in Western Art* (1967, reissued 1979).

The process of arranging music for particular instruments and combinations of instruments is discussed in Howard Mayer Brown, *Sixteenth-Century Instrumentation: The Music for the Florentine Intermedii* (1973); Claude V. Palisca, *Baroque Music*, 3rd ed. (1991), surveying the seminal period in the development of concerted music; Adam Carse, *The History of Orchestration* (1925, reissued 1964); Hector Berlioz, *Treatise on Instrumentation*, rev. and enlarged by Richard Strauss (1948; originally published in French, 1844); Nicolas Rimsky-Korsakow (Nikolay Rimsky-Korsakov), *Principles of Orchestration*, trans. from Russian (1923, reissued 1964); Michael Hurd, *The Orchestra* (1980); Madeau Stewart, *The Music Lover's Guide to the Instruments of the Orchestra* (1980); Joan Peyser (ed.), *The Orchestra: Origins and Transformations* (1986); and Mark C. Gridley and David Cutler, *Jazz Styles: History & Analysis*, 8th ed. (2003).

Current developments and research in the field are reflected in the articles of such special periodicals as *The Galpin Society Journal* (annual); *Journal of the American Musical Instrument Society* (annual); *The Musical Quarterly; Early Music* (quarterly); *Ethnomusicology* (3/yr.); and *Asian Music* (semiannual).

Historical surveys on the violin family, together with information on sound production in different types of instruments, are found in Martha Maas and Jane McIntosh Snyder, *Stringed Instruments of Ancient Greece* (1989); Hortense Panum, *The Stringed Instruments of the Middle Ages, Their Evolution and Development* (1939, reprinted 1971; originally published in Danish, 1915); Otto Andersson, *The Bowed-Harp: A Study in the History of Early Musical Instruments* (1930, reissued 1973; originally published in Swedish, 1923); Werner Bachmann, *The Origins of Bowing and the Development of Bowed Instruments Up to the Thirteenth Century* (1969; originally published in German, 2nd ed., 1966); and Mary Remnant, *English Bowed Instruments from Anglo-Saxon to Tudor Times* (1986). The most important family among Western stringed instruments is described and analyzed in David D. Boyden et al., *The New Grove Violin Family* (1989; also published as *Violin Family*); and Sheila M. Nelson, *The Violin and Viola* (1972). Henry Rasof, *The Folk, Country, and Bluegrass Musician's Catalogue* (1982), provides good coverage of 11 stringed folk instruments. For separate instruments, see Roslyn Rensch, *Harps and Harpists* (1989), a history with analysis of the instrument design and schools of playing; Joan Rimmer, *The Irish Harp*, 3rd ed. (1984); Susan Palmer and Samuel Palmer, *The Hurdy-Gurdy* (1980), a useful account of this little-studied instrument; Pandora Hopkins, *Aural Thinking in Norway: Performance and Communication with the Hardingfele* (1986), a thorough, original study; R.H. van Gulik, *The Lore of the Chinese Lute: An Essay in Ch'in Ideology*, new rev. ed. (1969); John Henry Felix, Leslie Nunes, and Peter F. Senecal, *The Ukulele: A Portuguese Gift to Hawaii* (1980); James Tyler and Paul Sparks, *The Early Mandolin* (1989); William R. Cumpiano and Jonathan D. Natelson, *Guitarmaking, Tradition and Technology: A Complete Reference for the Design and Construction of the Steel-String Folk Guitar and the Classical Guitar* (1987); José Romanillos, *Antonio de Torres, Guitar Maker: His Life and Work* (1987); and David Russell Young, *The Steel String Guitar: Construction & Repair*, updated ed. (1987).

MUSICAL NOTATION

Willi Apel, *The Notation of Polyphonic Music, 900–1600*, 5th ed. (1961), a standard textbook, including staff notation and tablatures, and many facsimiles used as exercises for transcription; Erhard Karkoschka, *Das Schriftbild der neuen Musik* (1966), an excellently documented study of contemporary notation; Walter Kaufmann, *Musical Notations of the Orient: Notational Systems of Continental East, South and*

Central Asia (1967); Carl Parrish, *The Notation of Medieval Music* (1957), excellent facsimiles; Emanuel Winternitz, *Musical Autographs from Monteverdi to Hindemith* (1955), a study of musical handwriting, with many facsimiles.

RHYTHM

Curt Sachs, *Rhythm and Tempo* (1953), the most comprehensive work on rhythm in music, ranges over many non-Western cultures as well as over the successive periods of Western musical history. Detailed rhythmical analyses of Western music since the 17th century appear in Grosvenor W. Cooper and Leonard B. Meyer, *The Rhythmic Structure of Music* (1960). Studies of special periods are available in Charles F. Abdy Williams, *The Aristoxenian Theory of Musical Rhythm* (1911); W.F. Jackson Knight, *St. Augustine's De Musica: A Synopsis* (1949); William G. Waite, *The Rhythm of Twelfth-Century Polyphony, Its Theory and Practice* (1954); Philip F. Radcliffe, "The Relation of Rhythm and Tonality in the Sixteenth Century," *Proc. R. Musical Assn.*, 57:73–97 (1931); and Henry D. Cowell, *New Musical Resources* (1930, reprinted 1969). Particular applications of rhythm have been studied in Charles F. Abdy Williams, *The Rhythm of Song* (1925); and William Thomson, *The Rhythm of Speech* (1923). Aesthetic aspects are considered in Margaret Glyn, *The Rhythmic Conception of Music* (1907); and Mathis Lussy, *Le Rythme musical*, 3rd ed. rev. (1897; abridged Eng. trans., *A Short Treatise on Musical Rhythm*, 1909). Émile Jaques-Dalcroze, *Le Rythme, la musique et l'éducation* (1920; Eng. trans., *Rhythm, Music and Education*, 1921), is the pioneer work in its aspect of the field; musical rhythm has been put in wider perspective by Elsie Fogerty, *Rhythm* (1937).

SCALES

Curt Sachs, *The Wellsprings of Music*, ed. by Jaap Kunst (1965), a systematic study of rudimentary scale types throughout the world and their evolution; Bruno Nettl, *Music in Primitive Culture* (1956), a concise and authoritative introduction to scale types and their geographical distribution; William P. Malm, *Music Cultures of the Pacific, the Near East, and Asia* (1967), lucid summaries of scale systems in non-Western art-music traditions; John L. Dunk, *The Structure of the Musical Scale* (1940), a thorough description of the diatonic scale; Antoine Auda, *Les Gammes musicales* (1947), a classic, comprehensive study of the history of scales in Western art music.

MUSICAL SOUND

Willem A. Van Bergeijk, J.R. Pierce, and E.A. David, *Waves and the Ear* (1960); Arthur H. Benade, *Horns, Strings and Harmony* (1960); Charles A. Culver, *Musical Acoustics*, 4th ed. (1956); John Backus, *The Acoustical Foundations of Music* (1969); John Mills, *A Fugue in Cycles and Bels* (1935); Max F. Meyer, *How We Hear: How Tones*

Make Music (1950); Llewelyn S. Lloyd, *The Musical Ear* (1940); Alexander Wood, *The Physics of Music*, 6th ed. (1962); René Descartes, *Musicae compendium* (1650; Eng. trans., *Compendium of Music*, 1961); Cornelis J. Nederveen, *Acoustical Aspects of Woodwind Instruments* (1969).

WESTERN MUSIC

General music reference works include Don Michael Randel (ed.), *The New Harvard Dictionary of Music* (1986); and Denis Arnold, *The New Oxford Companion to Music*, 2 vol. (1983, reprinted 1990). Also useful are Friedrich Blume (ed.), *Die Musik in Geschichte und Gegenwart*, 17 vol. (1949–86); Stanley Sadie (ed.), *The New Grove Dictionary of Music and Musicians*, 20 vol. (1980, reprinted 1993); and Theodore Baker, *Baker's Biographical Dictionary of Musicians*, 8th ed., rev. by Nicolas Slonimsky (1992).

Survey histories include Donald Jay Grout and Claude V. Palisca, *A History of Western Music*, 4th ed. (1988); *New Oxford History of Music*, 10 vol. (1954–90), with some volumes in 2nd editions; and K Marie Stolba, *The Development of Western Music: A History*, 2nd ed. (1994).

The *Prentice Hall History of Music Series* offers a comprehensive set of period surveys, including Jeremy Yudkin, *Music in Medieval Europe* (1989); Howard Mayer Brown, *Music in the Renaissance* (1976); Claude V. Palisca, *Baroque Music*, 3rd ed. (1991); Reinhard G. Pauly, *Music in the Classic Period*, 3rd ed. (1988); Rey M. Longyear, *Nineteenth-century*

Romanticism in Music, 3rd ed. (1988); and Eric Salzman, *Twentieth-century Music*, 3rd ed. (1988). The following monographs offer more detailed studies of specific periods: Albrecht Riethmüller and Frieder Zaminer (eds.), *Die Musik des Altertums* (1989); Lise Manniche, *Music and Musicians in Ancient Egypt* (1991); Giovanni Comotti, *Music in Greek and Roman Culture* (1989; originally published in Italian, 1979); Richard H. Hoppin, *Medieval Music* (1978); Gustave Reese, *Music in the Renaissance*, rev. ed. (1959); Lorenzo Bianconi, *Music in the Seventeenth Century* (1987; originally published in 1982); Manfred F. Bukofzer, *Music in the Baroque Era, from Monteverdi to Bach* (1947, reissued 1977); Philip G. Downs, *Classical Music* (1992); Leon Plantinga, *Romantic Music* (1984); Robert P. Morgan, *Twentieth-century Music* (1991); and Nicolas Slonimsky, *Music Since 1900*, 5th ed. (1994).

ALTERNATIVE ROCK

Eric Weisbard, "Introduction: What Is Alternative Rock?," in Eric Weisbard and Craig Marks (eds.), *Spin Alternative Record Guide* (1995), pp. vii–xii, discusses bands before, during, and after the alternative moment, with special emphasis on marginal and college-era practitioners; the essay also emphasizes "alternative sensibilities." Alan Cross, *The Alternative Music Almanac* (1995); and Pat Blashill and Michael Lavine, *Noise from the Underground* (1996), cover the history of alternative music.